Will Work for Holiness

Holiness and Righteousness – Is There a Difference?

by John Klein
with Michael Christopher

Lost in Translation
PO Box 8224
Bend, OR 97708

For speaking and conference information:
Lost in Translation
PO Box 8224
Bend, OR 97708
www.lostintranslation.org

Published by Lost in Translation.
© 2016 by John Klein with Michael Christopher

ISBN-13: 978-1523752188
ISBN-10: 1523752181

Cover design by Katie Klein
Email: katiecklein@ymail.com

Contents

Introduction

Torah. It's an interesting word, but most of us don't have a clue as to what it means — or even its origin. The movie buffs among us might at least recall the film by that name, with the same word repeated three times. You know: Tora, Tora, Tora.

That title was the Japanese code word used to indicate that complete surprise had been achieved when their naval forces reached the Hawaiian Islands to begin their attack on Pearl Harbor in 1941. *Tora* (虎, pronounced tòɾá) literally means "tiger." But in this case it was an acronym for **to**tsugeki **ra**igeki (突擊雷擊), which means "lightning attack."[1]

However, its first use was not in the Japanese language. Its origins lie much farther back in antiquity, in the very first language spoken by man. The same language that God created and gave to the first couple, Adam and Eve, to use: Hebrew. This is also the language God chose to use in writing His Word, the Bible. Scholars estimate that over 90% of the biblical text was originally written using Hebrew, with only a scattering of Aramaic and Greek used mostly in the book of Daniel and the writings of Paul in the New Testament respectively.[2]

So, the word Torah is therefore a Hebrew word and is used extensively in the biblical text. However, almost always it is interpreted into English as "Law."

I think this is very unfortunate. The word does mean "Law," but it also means so much more.

In many biblical passages, such as Deuteronomy 29:21, 30:10, and 31:26, the first five books of the Old Testament are called by God the "Book of the Law" (Torah). These are the only books in the Bible, with the exception of Revelation, that were written down by the "writer" after hearing spoken words from the very mouth of God.

All the others were inspired to be written as the Spirit of God moved on the writer, or as the writer recounted a vision or dream he had witnessed. In other cases the writer was given the interpretation directly by God, which he then wrote down as a portend of some imminent, major event.

But either way — whether the human "author" wrote down exactly what God told him to write, or relied entirely on God-given inspiration — our Bible has long been the most frequently purchased book in the world. There are many reasons for that phenomenon, not the least of which are the precise, original meanings literally embedded in dozens (hundreds?) of different passages, with the unlimited capacity to change the lives of millions of readers . . . for the better.

This book will focus on some of the most fascinating biblical passages, as dictated and/or inspired by God in the very language He created, for the single purpose of helping all of us understand precisely what He wanted us to know.

Chapter 1
How God Communicates with Man

It is generally understood that there are three
different levels of revelation, or communication,
that God can have with mankind. The clearest and
most direct is, of course, face-to-face. The second
level, but clearly not as direct and certainly open
more to interpretation by the recipient, is a vision or
a prophecy. However, I am not suggesting that any
prophecy or vision in the Bible is suspect or less
than accurate — I am making a distinction whose
importance will become clearer in the text that
follows.

God spoke face-to-face to clearly describe in detail
the truth with which He blessed mankind. For
example, most of the face-to-face information we
have from the very mouth of God, contained in the
first five books of the Bible, includes detailed
instructions on how we are to conduct our lives and
make covenant, both with Him and with others.
How to bring blessing to ourselves and others, and
how to put smiles on the face of our Creator, are all
communicated to us from a face-to-face encounter
involving Moses and God, so we would get it perfect.

The third way God chose to communicate, which is
also represented in His Word, is by having His Spirit
move on people and literally inspire them to record
His message. Examples of this would include the

book of Psalms, or many of the New Testament letters written by the Apostles to various congregations. There is no face-to-face encounter, inspiring the writer to preserve words directly dictated by God, nor is there a supernatural revelation, such as a vision or prophecy, to be carefully described by the author.

The Construction of the Old and the New Testament

The Old and the New Testaments are built in somewhat the same fashion. Both have a section that represents the very words of God, either being directly dictated to the writer or via the writer's personal relationship (or confrontation) with God. In the latter case the writer extensively quotes what God has revealed to him, by writing down God's very words or by including his own paraphrase in the resulting text. Obviously the first five books of the Old Testament and the four Gospels in the New Testament all fall into this category.

Each of the Old and the New Testaments also include prophetic portions, sometimes resulting in whole books dedicated to visions and portends about future events. Books such as Isaiah, Jeremiah, and Joel come to mind in the Old Testament, and whole sections of books such as First and Second Thessalonians — plus the entire book of Revelation — are all excellent examples in the New Testament. The inspirational examples would include the books of Psalms and Proverbs in the Old Testament, and the letters written by the apostles in the New Testament.

Thus in the Bible's very construction we can see how God chooses to speak to mankind. Also, in our own lives and relationships with God we can sometimes observe these same methods of interaction. Of course face-to-face is rare, but if and when it happens you would certainly sit up (or perhaps fall flat on your face!) and take much more notice than you might after waking up from a dream or feeling the direct inspiration of God, suggesting some insight about what you should think or do. Yes, they are all important, but face-to-face interaction would certainly catch our attention more than the other means of communication.

In fact, in the busyness of our world and the distractions it contains, or because of some of the teachings from our church leaders today, many of us don't even believe in dreams or visions. Or at best, we give them only a slight bit of attention. Usually we discard them by assuming they're the result of something we ate the night before, never stopping to consider that God might be trying to get our attention.

Even worse is our attentiveness to the moves of the Spirit as He tries to make direct suggestions for our lives. The most common complaint I get from people who believe they have a very poor relationship with their creator is the comment that they almost never hear from God. However, the problem lies not with God Himself, but rather, with their inability to hear Him. In the current age we tend to sweep away as irrelevant what appear to be random thoughts that upon more serious consideration make a lot of sense. These thoughts, so often quickly discarded and ignored, are many times the very thoughts of our Lord trying to give us needed instructions and guidance.

Unfortunately, we have learned to not hear these words, and so we discard them without consideration. Along with the reading of God's Word, this is the primary way God communicates with us on a day-to-day basis, but we have trained ourselves to ignore God's voice. And we certainly have not learned to respond back when He does talk to us. Remember, He communicated to Moses in that still small voice, and so, too, with us. His people can hear His voice, and we will need to be able to do just that when the things that are about to come into our lives and upon the world start occurring, as many end-times biblical prophecies begin to unfold and come to their consummation.

The point is that face-to-face communications stand out more than other forms of communication, and are much more likely to be heard and understood by the recipient. That is why many biblical scholars recognize the importance of Torah first, and then the four Gospels. All the remaining communications to mankind found in the Bible, and certainly our own ideas about what we think we have heard from God, are always — or at least should be — in submission to these foundational face-to-face instructions that came directly from God Himself.

For most of us this point seems obvious, yet sometimes we still go about living our lives while completely ignoring it. We allow our emotions to govern our decisions. The whim of the moment usually wins the day, and we give very little attention to God's written instructions that would help us make our day-to-day decisions, as was God's original intention. The phrase "I feel that God is saying" is prioritized over "It is written." We specialize in being very much in touch with our personal feelings and desires rather than in studying God's Word, so as to be very much in touch with His standard and therefore allowing it to be our foundation.

Truth does not waiver over time, and is not subject to changes brought about by our emotions. That is why God did not base His promises of blessing to us on how we feel about things. Rather, He based them on fixed ideals that need no modification through time, and no changes in social order or values. Today we are often taught a "living document concept" which presents to us the idea that our United States Constitution, or worse, the Bible, needs to be understood not from ancient perspectives, such as the original writers intended, but rather from our own or the currently accepted social values. The common statement is, "Oh, that idea is outdated." But is it really?

Knowing then the importance of Torah, the first five books of our Bible, we should be experts on these texts first, right? We should study the rest with the understanding that none of the other biblical books, and the information and instructions contained within them, should contradict the foundational Torah. When it appears that they do (and I agree that sometimes they do indeed), this calls for further study of both the foundational and the extra-foundational passages to enable us to come to the correct conclusion.

A Special Blessing or a Curse

There are some interesting passages in Deuteronomy that make this point clear.

> "You shall not add to the word which I am commanding you, nor take away from it, that you may keep the commandments of the LORD your God which I command you. (Dueteronomy 4:2)

> "Whatever I command you, you shall be careful to do; you shall not add to nor take away from it. (Deuteronomy 12:32)

These verses are then followed up by passages such as this:

> See, I am setting before you today a blessing and a curse: the blessing, if you listen to the commandments of the LORD your God, which I am commanding you today; and the curse, if you do not listen to the commandments of the LORD your God, but turn aside from the way which I am commanding you today, by following other gods which you have not known. (Deuteronomy 11:26–28)

These face-to-face communications and instructions that God gave to His people are set apart by importance and priority. Nowhere else in the Bible does God give instructions with such emphasis, with one exception: the book of Revelation. Nowhere else does God warn us to not make additions or subtractions to His words. God is emphasizing the importance and pointing to the foundation of truth by these warnings.

So — what are exactly the truths that we should not be making changes to? In all of the contexts of these verses, such as Deuteronomy 11, we see that it is the face-to-face instructions that God gave to Moses that we find in the first five books of the Bible, as He further emphasized in Deuteronomy 29:21:

> These are the words of the covenant which the LORD commanded Moses to make with the sons of Israel in the land of Moab, besides the covenant which He had made with them at Horeb.

Therefore the reader of any biblical text should realize that the key to understanding any particular passage should be Torah, or the gospels in the New Testament. However, it is also important to remember that the face-to-face communications that Yeshua/Jesus recorded in those New Testament texts were mostly commentaries on Torah, as this passage from Matthew makes perfectly clear:

> "I haven't come to abolish the Torah but to fulfill or to properly understand Torah." (Matthew 5:17)

Chapter 2
The Meaning of Torah

In my other books I have mentioned that the Hebrew language and letters (of which there are 22) are unique among the many world scripts. All the other lettering systems of the world are phonic, meaning that each letter in other alphabets presents to the reader a sound. In order to read the words that are formed in that written language, all you need to know, for the most part, is the sound that each letter makes. Thus most of the western languages are phonic driven.

However, in the eastern part of the world, especially in their original form, many lettering systems provided letters that were pictographs. They did not suggest a way to pronounce themselves, but rather they provided a concept to be understood, usually through a picture. Those cave pictures we see in the Americas, drawn by ancient peoples, do not suggest that their authors were slow and usually poor artists as well. Instead they were writing in a pictographic language, one toward which our western minds are simply not oriented.

A Standout and Unique Language

Hebrew is different and unique among all other languages. Each of its letters presents to the reader both a *phonic sound* and a *pictographic concept*. So this language tells you how to pronounce each word

while it also provides pictographic concepts that —
taken together and in context — tell what each word
means. Thus in Hebrew, when a word contains a
certain letter that word also conveys the idea of that
letter. The same is therefore true with the 90% of
the Bible that was originally written in that same
language.

In my other books I have gone into some detail
about the above, such as *Lost in Translation:
Rediscovering the Hebrew Roots of Our Faith*. But
to give one example here, the Hebrew word *Satan* is
spelled via three Hebrew letters: *sin, tet,* and *noon*.
We know what that word means in English because
we have been taught its meaning. But in the
pictographs no teaching is required. Thus, in
Hebrew pictographs the word "Satan" means the
"snake that consumes life." Notice I didn't say
"consumed," because beginning with Adam and Eve
that is exactly what Satan has been doing. As we
listen to him, bondage and sin are ushered into our
lives and Satan is more than happy to steal our God-
given identity and God-given authority and thereby
consume our very lives.

Back to Torah

But what is the pictographic message that God has
embedded in the word *Torah*? This is where it gets
interesting. The Bible's first five books, and
especially the face-to-face messages God has given
to us, are indeed special. Torah is spelled *tav, vav,
resh, hey*. These four pictographs convey this

meaning: "Behold the man nailed to the cross." How New Testament is that message . . . but here it is in the Old! Unfortunately for the English reader, the word "Torah" almost always gets interpreted as "Law."

To my mind this is a major misdirection. Yes, the Torah does contain the Laws of God. Nowhere else does God delineate His principles for holy living. And yes, you will find them repeated in other books in the Old and New Testaments, but nowhere else are those Laws listed and clearly laid out. When laws are mentioned in other places they are not presented in an additive way, but rather in a confirmatory way.

This rule of neither adding nor subtracting to God's Law, as presented in Torah, is obeyed by God as well. He lives in a way that is exemplary. He does not live exceptionally. Today in the church, a typical phrase often used, is "What would Jesus (Yeshua) do?" Well, we now know the answer. As He lived on earth two thousand years ago, He still lives . . . and that is according to His Torah. Remember, when he was in front of His accusers they had to make up lies because they couldn't find anything that He had done against the Laws of Moses in the Torah.

Also recall that, in Revelation 4, John experiences a visit to heaven in which he sees God sitting on his throne with other beings around the throne. And what are these beings communicating? They are describing how God is living by saying, "Holy, holy,

holy is the Lord God almighty who was, and is, and is to come."

The implication is that if God was holy — and is holy — He will also be holy in the future. In other words, God is currently living His live in a holy fashion, modeling for us how we should live.

Behold the Man Nailed to the Cross

I find it most interesting that embedded within the Hebrew word for the Law of God is a prophecy about who He is and what He would someday do. Another pictographic meaning could also be "Behold the man nailed to the sign of the covenant." By reading my first book most of you have now become acquainted with the concept of covenant and its prevalence in the Bible. In both the Old and the New Testaments it is evident to all that God is a covenant-making Creator. He loves to establish covenant with us, and He loves it even more when we covenant back with Him.

Recall that a simple definition of covenant is "relationship," and relationship lies at the very heart of God. The sign of the covenant contained the promise that God made at the very beginning, upon our fall into sin. He told us that He could fix our predicament which, of course, was death, the penalty for our sin. He would pay the price, the curse of the Law, of Torah, by offering up Himself on the sign, the Cross. He became our Passover Lamb and took away the penalty for not following Torah and the Law that it contains.

Now some propose that He came to die on the Cross to take away the Law, doing away with it once and for all and substituting grace. Is this true? Or did his death just take away the penalty or the curse of the Law of Torah?

We will address that question in this book, but it will be more fully answered in a future book, the focus of which will be the applicability of the Laws of God. We will attempt to determine whether the Laws of God have been abolished and replaced by grace. Or, are they still applicable and is God still calling us to obey them?

I hope you find that the explanation presented in that book will give you added insight and a more complete understanding of God's Word. However, before we begin the study of whether Torah is still applicable we need to come to a better understanding of two words that most of us would define as synonyms; that is, as two words meaning basically the same thing. But do they really? I propose that in today's English, perhaps they do. But in biblical Hebrew, not at all.

These two words are "righteousness" and "holiness."

Chapter 3
What Does It Mean to Be Righteous?

For the moment, let us draw our attention to the following verses in John 3:1–10:

> Now there was a man of the Pharisees, named Nicodemus, a ruler of the Jews; this man came to Jesus by night and said to Him, "Rabbi, we know that You have come from God *as* a teacher; for no one can do these signs that You do unless God is with him." Jesus answered and said to him, "Truly, truly, I say to you, unless one is born again he cannot see the kingdom of God."

> Nicodemus said to Him, "How can a man be born when he is old? He cannot enter a second time into his mother's womb and be born, can he?" Jesus answered, "Truly, truly, I say to you, unless one is born of water and the Spirit he cannot enter into the kingdom of God. "That which is born of the flesh is flesh, and that which is born of the Spirit is spirit. "Do not be amazed that I said to you, 'You must be born again.' "The wind blows where it wishes and you hear the sound of it, but do not know where it comes from and where it is going; so is everyone who is born of the Spirit." Nicodemus said to Him, "How can these things be?" Jesus answered and said to him, "Are you the teacher of Israel and do not understand these things?

The first thing that strikes me is that the appointed teachers of Torah to God's people did not understand these things. In other words, Yeshua was disgruntled that His appointed teachers did not have a grasp of something that should have been a basic tenet, as understood from His Word. And that word was the *only* word He had given to His people up to that point, which was Torah and the rest of the books contained in the *Tanakh* . . . or the Old Testament (of course, these instructions were not called the Old Testament during Yeshua's life on earth).

That Yeshua was disgruntled tells us that what God is saying here in this chapter, about rebirth and salvation, was nothing new. They should have known this! It is foundational. The new man is one that is born of flesh and born of spirit.

Born of the Spirit

John 3:6 introduces us to a phrase that has been misunderstood by the church.

That which is born of the flesh is flesh, and that which is born of the spirit is spirit.

The phrase "born of the flesh," above, is easy to understand. It refers to our physical existence as created by God. But "born of the spirit" has been misunderstood. Many think that God is contrasting "born of the flesh" with having a body, and "born of the spirit" as not having a body. This is not true. I Corinthians 15:41-50 tells us:

The sun has one kind of splendor, the moon another and the stars another; and star differs from star in splendor. 42 So will it be with the resurrection of the dead. The body that is sown is perishable, it is raised imperishable; 43 it is sown in dishonor, it is raised in glory; it is sown in weakness, it is raised in power; [44] it is sown a natural body, it is raised a spiritual body.

If there is a natural body, there is also a spiritual body. [45] So it is written: "The first man Adam became a living being"; the last Adam, a life-giving spirit. [46] The spiritual did not come first, but the natural, and after that the spiritual. [47] The first man was of the dust of the earth; the second man is of heaven. [48] As was the earthly man, so are those who are of the earth; and as is the heavenly man, so also are those who are of heaven. [49] And just as we have borne the image of the earthly man, so shall we bear the image of the heavenly man. [50] I declare to you, brothers and sisters, that flesh and blood cannot inherit the kingdom of God, nor does the perishable inherit the imperishable.

In verse 44 above, you'll notice that it talks about our natural body just like our passage in John 3 did, but it also says that this natural body will be raised as a spiritual body. And it then says, "If there is a natural body there is a spiritual body." Obviously, the verse is instructing that there are both natural bodies and spiritual bodies, of which God's people will inherit the latter once God returns. Both the Greek word for body (*soma*), and the Hebrew word for body (*bashar*), mean physical bodies, the kind of bodies that living creatures have.

Notice that this word "body" is used to inform us, in I Corinthians 15, that the natural as well as the spiritual being will have a physical body. The natural body is distinct from the spiritual body. The spiritual body does not represent some sort of mystical, non-physical state of being, but rather, as the quotation above says, the physical and spiritual bodies vary in attributes.

One is perishable; the other is imperishable. One is sown in dishonor; the other is raised in glory. One is weak; the other is powerful. One is born of the image of the earth; the other is born of the image of the heavenlies. One cannot inherit the kingdom of God; the other can.

Listen, I tell you a mystery: We will not all sleep, but we will all be changed — 52 in a flash, in the twinkling of an eye, at the last trumpet. For the trumpet will sound, the dead will be raised imperishable, and we will be changed. 53 For the perishable must clothe itself with the imperishable, and the mortal with immortality. 54 When the perishable has been clothed with the imperishable, and the mortal with immortality, then the saying that is written will come true: "Death has been swallowed up in victory."
(I Corinthians 15:52–54)

And the verses that follow our first quote above explain that, after the second coming of our Messiah, all those who believe and trust and rely for their salvation through their faith, receive their spiritual bodies. We do not become disembodied spirits. The implications of the fact that spirits also have bodies may apply more than just to mankind, but also to angels as well as to devils, and as well as to God Himself.

Today, however, many of us have the same reaction as Nicodemus, because we don't understand what this rebirth is all about and what it accomplishes for us. To be born again is an invitation to become a member of God's family, just like we were before mankind fell into sin. This was the original state of mankind. We were made in our Creator's image. Our natures were the same. We looked like Him, we thought like Him, and we acted in accord with the same set of standards.

When Sin Entered the World

However, when sin entered the world because we chose to violate His standards, we fell from God's perfect state and from God's family. We had chosen to do our own thing. Thus we had created our own family. Well, actually not our "own" family — we had joined Satan's family! Unfortunately, the destiny of this family has always been death.

What salvation is really all about is mending this divorce and reuniting us with God through the process of being reborn, making us one again with Him. But in the process we do not reunite the old family's attributes with God's family, especially mankind's attribute of sin and death. This rebirth leaves the penalty of our sin behind. Death is done away with because our sin has been paid for by someone else. And we know who paid that price: none other than Yeshua Himself.

This rebirth is as though we are allowed to be grafted into the family of God again. Or maybe it's more similar to the idea of being adopted into a new family and leaving the old behind. When someone is adopted, the best results are had when the adopted son or daughter leaves behind their old ways and takes on the characteristics of their new family. But whatever happens, the family addition will now be recognized by others as a member of the adopted family, and they will acquire the family's name. This is what James 1:21–25 is all about:

> Therefore, putting aside all filthiness and *all* that remains of wickedness, in humility receive the word implanted, which is able to save your souls. But prove yourselves doers of the word, and not merely hearers who delude themselves. For if anyone is a hearer of the word and not a doer, he is like a man who looks at his natural face in a mirror; for *once* he has looked at himself and gone away, he has immediately forgotten what kind of person he was. But one who looks intently at the perfect law, the *law* of liberty, and abides by it, not having become a forgetful hearer but an effectual doer, this man will be blessed in what he does.

Here we see James referring to the Word. We see that it has the ability to save our souls. Also, we are instructed to be doers of the word and not just hearers. Then the text goes on to describe a person who is a hearer but not a doer, and James calls that person deluded — someone who looks at himself in the mirror, but upon turning away from the mirror immediately forgets what he looks like or who he really is. But James then tells us what the Word is.

That Word is the Law of God. The underlying Hebrew word here for "Law" is Torah, the first five books of the Old Testament. He is making the case for the Torah being the foundation for our identity. Remember, the first century believers could not have access to the New Testament because it didn't exist yet. So whenever you see the word "Word," or "Scriptures," and even sometimes "Law," the writer is specifically referring to either the first five books (the Torah) or the *Tanakh* (the rest of the Old Testament).

This metaphor is saying that we are adopted into a new family upon being saved. And these family members live their lives in ways that are immediately recognizable by the whole community. Their lifestyle may be very different from the lifestyle by which others in the community live. And, when the members of this family live this unique lifestyle the community can identify them all, as long as they are not just hearers but also doers.

What creates confusion is when someone with the family's name goes around acting like everyone else in the community, and ignores the lifestyle honored by the family. Others might say, "Who is this guy, really? He has the same name as our unique family but he doesn't act like one. He must be a hypocrite, or maybe a con artist pretending to be part of something when he really isn't."

This is the problem James is addressing. He is telling us that when we become reborn and become a member of a new family we should forget our old ways and focus on the standard our new family lives by. Otherwise, we will be accused of being hypocrites and con artists, and of denigrating the family's work and reputation.

Whether we realize it or not, upon being saved we are immediately adopted into the family and kingdom of God. We inherit His unique qualities and attributes. John 3:16 makes clear that the requirements for adoption are faith alone. No works are required here.

> For God so loved the world, that He gave His only begotten Son, that whoever believes in Him shall not perish, but have eternal life.

This word "believes" in the verse above, in Greek, is *pestyuo*. It means "to believe, to be persuaded of, to place confidence in." the Hebrew equivalent word is *emoonah*. This word means to "prop, to stay, to support, to bear in the arms." But the meaning I like best is "to be founded, firm, stable and trustworthy."

Becoming a believer through faith means that you become confident and stable in your newfound reliance on God, and your new identity with His kingdom. It does not mean waking up every day and wondering whether you are a child of the king. It implies a consistency of belief, trusting in your new Father to bring salvation.

Confirmation of Our Family Membership

In other words, faith isn't something you just think about but something that begins to guide and define your new life. It should permeate your being to the degree that you become stable and confident in your newfound identity and the destiny of your new family.

And so we should be! Romans 4 confirms the qualities and attributes that come along with this adoption into God's family.

> What then shall we say that Abraham, our forefather according to the flesh, has found? 2For if Abraham was justified by works, he had something to boast about, but not before God. 3For what does the Scripture say? "ABRAHAM BELIEVED GOD, AND IT WAS CREDITED TO HIM AS RIGHTEOUSNESS." Romans 4:1-3

Romans also makes it clear that works are nice, but they do not get you adopted into God's kingdom. This is one of the profound differences between the way God's kingdom works and all the other worldly religions. Doing good works, in most of the other religions in the world, will supposedly earn you rewards that usually include entry into a good place in the next life, or the equivalent of salvation in the Bible. The gods of these other religions require your obedience to them. And if you don't obey them explicitly you don't get an invite into this "better place" upon your death.

The religion of the God of the Bible offers to mankind a completely contrasting proposal. All we need for salvation and entry into God's "good place" in the hereafter is faith. I think that is why so many people reject this proposal. We seem to need to earn it. We can't just believe and trust in the work of someone else.

We need to justify ourselves by compensating for the poor choices we make, usually by doing something good. Then we feel better about ourselves. And in so doing we then think that we are able to offer those "good things" we've done to God as payments for entry into the good place the Bible calls heaven. Or, in the age to come.

Do We Really Go to Heaven?

In the church today it is common to hear teachings about our destiny after this life. We are told that someday we will all be with God in heaven. But is that really true? Is that the end game plan that God has for His people?

It is only true in the very short term. Until he comes back, following Yeshua's death on the Cross, all those who have believed in Yeshua before their death will have gone to be with God in heaven. But this is only very shortsighted. After the Messiah comes back, all of that will change and God's long-term plans will begin to be fulfilled. And that does not include dwelling in heaven, but dwelling on earth.

For the first 1000 years it will be essentially the same old earth. God purified it at the beginning of the first 1000 years, by removing the beast and the impurities that his followers introduced into His creation. But at the end of the 1000-year reign, the text in Revelation tells us that He will make a new earth. By understanding the Bible as describing the complete plan of God, we understand that his goal is to restore the earth back to the way it was before man fell. We don't know too much about the post-

1000-year earthly state of being, but we do know that it will be perfect. And, it will be our home . . . not heaven.

What God says is that the payment for our sin has already been paid by Him. All we need to do is accept the payment, with gratitude, and trust Him with a repentant heart. And this includes relying on Him and His guarantee to take care of us in the age to come.

This faith ushers in something else as well. Verse three in the passage from Romans above says that righteousness was credited to Abraham through his faith. It seems that righteousness is the quality that sets God's people apart. Is this a certain quality about our spirit, something we might inherit, maybe? It is definitely not something we earn by being good. It is given to us because of our faith and reliance on God. Thus the author of Romans is saying that God's people are inherently righteous. And we *look* righteous because, by conforming our lives to *His* ways we *act* like it, too.

Righteousness — What Is it, Really?

It is clear that we are called to be righteous, especially in light of Matthew 25:46. In referring to unbelievers it says, "these shall go away into everlasting punishment: but the righteous into life eternal." It seems to make a big difference in God's eyes whether someone is righteous or not. This should be a big motivator for us to figure out exactly what this thing called "righteousness" really is.

The Hebrew word for righteousness is *zedak*. It is spelled *zadee, dalet, coof*. It is used in the sense of something that is true, just, and right. It is also used of God and His angels, and in regard to God's people who are sacred to Him. It also means "to be straight."

In several places in the biblical text God chooses to call His people *yeshurun*. This word can be found in the original Hebrew text of Deuteronomy 32:15 and 33:5, 26. It is a tender, loving appellation or endearment, used by God in describing His people, Israel. It means "straight, level, esteemed as right, approved."

I find the use of this word interesting in light of the fact that usually His people — us — are many times not acting or thinking straight, and actually deserve no esteem or approval from God. I think God sees our potential. He has the ability to esteem us through the forgiveness that came from the work of His Son, Yeshua. In light of Psalms 14:3 and Romans 3:12, which communicate to us that "no one is good, no not one," we really do need His forgiveness. But God is also able to see the quality of righteousness we inherited through faith as well. He does know how to identify those who are His. No works required there — just a name change and a change in our nature.

Born Again?

Have you ever wondered why God uses the idea of being born again when He talks about salvation and the faith it requires? Maybe it's true. Righteousness is inherited because the spirit of our new inherited nature is made whole, and because we now acquire one of the attributes of our new family — righteousness. So, when we leave behind the old inheritance and receive a new inheritance, the new quality of righteousness is had through faith. This understanding really helps when trying to comprehend James 1:23–25:

> For if anyone is a hearer of the word and not a doer, he is like a man who looks at his natural face in a mirror; 24 for *once* he has looked at himself and gone away, he has immediately forgotten what kind of person he was. 25 But one who looks intently at the perfect law, the *law* of liberty, and abides by it, not having become a forgetful hearer but an effectual doer, this man will be blessed in what he does.

We have a new identity when we become a believer. James equates that new identity with the "perfect Law." The perfect Law is what we are supposed to look like. We have a new nature, righteousness. And that is the image we see when we look in the mirror. We now look like our Maker. Remember, we were created in His image. The Torah, the Law, and God are all referred to as light, so it is not surprising that the image we now see of ourselves is called the "perfect Law."

God and His word are supposed to light our way, leading us to Him and His righteousness. His family is identified by the qualities and attributes of being righteous, because the definition of righteousness is to be straight. And now, through faith, we are inherently straight even though we still struggle with sin.

Betrothal and Righteousness

[20] Here I am! I stand at the door and knock. If anyone hears my voice and opens the door, I will come in and eat with that person, and they with me. [21] To the one who is victorious, I will give the right to sit with me on my throne, just as I was victorious and sat down with my Father on his throne. (Revelation 3:20–21)

The church today interprets the verses above to mean that God is standing at the door of our hearts, asking us if He can come in and dwell there. This is a classic salvation passage, referring to our process of becoming righteous via faith. But is there something more?

As we have explained in our previous writings, the concept of salvation is basic to our lives and our relationships with our king and groom. Standing at the door and knocking was a widely understood phrase by Hebrews living during the first century. This passage was referencing what the groom and His father would do in order to make a marriage proposal. If the door was opened by the potential bride, they would come in and drink the first of four cups of wine, three that would be drunk that evening and the fourth at the wedding itself, usually months later.

As we have learned in our other writings, these four cups paralleled the concept of covenant and included contractual obligations of the groom as well as the bride. These obligations always included, for the bride, to maintain her purity. And for us today, what these obligations represent is us being straight. And the concept of being "straight" in the Bible is associated with righteousness.

Chapter 4
How Do We Walk in a Straight Way?

Righteousness is an inherent quality we acquire through faith in God. God is righteous, and He gives us this attribute and makes it part of our natural being, just like He is. This is one of the reasons why, when we become part of His family and inherit salvation through faith, we feel all the more convicted when we violate God's principals.

So what, then, is *holiness*?

Most of us think of righteousness and holiness as synonyms representing the same concept. That is where the confusion lies. In God's Word they are distinctly different. As we have learned, the word for righteousness is *zedak*, which we spelled out previously. In contrast, the word for holiness is *kadesh*. It is spelled *coof, dalet, shen,* and it means "holy and sacred."

But the meanings that mean the most to me are "set apart and pure." I can't get my head around holy or sacred. Those words just don't convey much to me other than maybe "being religious." The ideas conveyed in "set apart and pure" hit me right in the heart.

Let me explain. In the Bible, the idea of being set apart is used many times by God in describing His people. *Kahal* is the Hebrew word that God uses to refer to His people. Many times He used the idea of *assembly* or *congregation* of Israel, which was a gathering together of His people who were called out to be set apart from the nations. The word "nations," in this context, was contrasting those who were not believers with those who were. We are an assembly, called out and set apart by God for His purposes.

In biblical Hebrew thinking, the meaning of the word "Egypt" meant "the world" as in "fallen man." God's people were called out from Egypt to form a new nation in a promised land specifically set apart for them as they were set apart for God.

I can understand being set apart. My actions, my associations, the entertainment I involve myself with, the way I think, the way I act, my code of ethics — all should set me apart. This definition I can understand in a practical way.

I can also relate to purity in a practical way. From a Hebraic perspective, the concept of purity was used at the Tabernacle. Someone who would serve there and worship God would be required to make sure they were pure when doing so. This was represented metaphorically by having a large basin filled with water, called a *laver*, just before the entrance to the Inner Court. The priest who planned to enter would be required to purify himself by washing before entering into the presence of God. This washing represented what was going on in the heart of the priest. As he took the time to wash, he was also speaking with his God, asking for forgiveness and cleansing his inner being through repentance.

Also, this idea of purity was applicable to the sacrifices that were brought by God's people to be offered for their sins. Passages such as Exodus 12:5 and Leviticus 1:3, along with many others, instruct us to bring unblemished lambs or other sacrifices to the bronze altar at His tabernacle. In Malachi 1:14 God curses those who bring blemished animals to be offered to the Lord. The word for unblemished is *tamim*, which means "to be perfect and complete." It also meant "to be whole, upright in conduct, and blameless."

Why was this such a big deal to God? All of these sacrifices were calls to remember. They were not substitutes for Yeshua, the Lamb of God who was hung on the Cross. They never were given for the remission of sin.

As you may recall, God sacrificed the first animal in the Garden of Eden, which provided a covering for Adam and Eve. The fig leaves did not suffice. Only the blood of someone innocent could cover for their sins.

In this case the covering was provided by a lamb. This lamb's skin acted to cover over the result of Adam and Eve's act of rebellion against God's instruction not to eat of the tree of the knowledge of good and evil. That very day, that promise was fulfilled and they died.

However, understand that, in Hebrew thinking, death amounts to being separated from our creator. Adam and Eve's nakedness was a sign to them that the warning that God had given them, about not eating from the tree, would be fulfilled if they did so. They would die. This covering, however, intervened. But, it did not separate their sin from themselves; it only put a barrier between their sin and God.

All the sacrifices that God required his people to make later on did the same thing. No sacrifice ever separated the sin from the sinner because it never had such power. Mankind was still stuck with the death penalty. Only the last Adam, someone coming in the form of man to live a perfect life, could remove the sentence of death.

How was this perfect life measured? Against what standard or set of rules was the Messiah's perfection measured? Was it measured against some code that the Romans had erected? Was it the ancient code of Hammurabi, or some other code created by some other culture that existed at the same time?

No. It was the very code that God had given the Israelites to obey some 1500 years earlier, as it is recorded in the Tanach (i.e., the Old Testament).

> He will not always strive *with us*,
> Nor will He keep *His anger* forever.
> He has not dealt with us according to our sins,
> Nor rewarded us according to our iniquities.
> [11] For as high as the heavens are above the earth,
> So great is His lovingkindness toward those who fear Him.

12 As far as the east is from the west,
So far has He removed our transgressions from us.
13 Just as a father has compassion on *his* children,
So the LORD has compassion on those who fear Him.
(Psalm 103:9–13)

Here the psalmist informs us that we will not be judged according to our sins or iniquities, but according to God's great lovingkindness toward those who fear Him.

Here, the word "fear" is *yara*, which means "to be afraid, to reverence, to be upright because of your reverence for Him." Being upright implies that one puts forth effort to live a life that is holy. Thus we "fear the Lord" by obeying the Lord.

Old Testament Judgement Verses New Testament Grace?

The passage above, from the 103rd Psalm, refers to God's "lovingkindness." The underlying Hebrew word for lovingkindness is *Chesed*. This word is used 248 times in the Old Testament, many times in the same context that David is using it in this Psalm. That is, expressing God's mercy and grace for His people even though they fall short in their actions and their thinking, in accordance with His Law.

This contradicts some in the church today, who propose that the concept of grace and mercy is limited to the New Testament. They propose that Yeshua came and gave grace to man, in contrast to the Old Testament where God is said to be a God of

Judgment. So they call the God of the Old Testament a God of Judgment whereas the God of the New Testament is a God of Grace.

Nothing could be further from the truth. Unfortunately, this incorrect idea is generated by an inconsistency in translation of the same word. When the word *Chesed* is found in the Old Testament, many times it is translated as lovingkindness. On the other hand, in the New Testament, the same word (or its Greek equivalent) gets translated as "grace." This inconsistency helps perpetuate an incorrect understanding.

In contrast to the lambs and other sacrificial animals that were offered to provide a covering over our sin, God's sacrifice of His son provided the means to remove our sin altogether. In fact, it's as far as the east is from the west. Thus, because of the price the Messiah paid on the Cross, we become white as snow.

These sacrifices were given only as a covering over for our sin, and a remembrance of the promise of the future coming of the Lamb to give of Himself, thus becoming our payment for our sin. Because He was perfect, whole, and upright, so should our offering to Him be.

Today there is no Temple, making it impossible for us to present sacrifices. The sacrifice that we offer to God now is our will. We offer up our will and our lives, conforming them to His will. So, when we are tempted to violate the Laws of God, to be holy is to reject our will, sacrificing it and replacing it with behavior that is pure and lines up with the Law of God.

Our obedience to God should not be rote, going through the motions only, without a heartfelt, repentant, humble attitude. When we approach God, asking for forgiveness, knowing full well that we're just going to turn around again and commit the same sin again, it is similar to offering up blemished lambs. And He doesn't approve.

Nor should we give half-hearted offerings that reflect what is left over. For example, our tithe should come from the first part of our earnings, not from what is left over at the end of the month after we pay our other bills.

The practical application comes when we ask for His forgiveness in regard to a specific sin. Do we then do our part? As Psalm 103:12 explains:

> As far as the east is from the west, so far has He removed our transgressions from us.

Our responsibility is to then walk away from these temptations by saying, "No, I'm not thinking about that nor am I doing that anymore, period." God does understand that sometime we fail even in our efforts to change our lives, but over time, if we are persistent in making the effort to do well, we will win the battle.

So, the idea of holiness is to set ourselves apart by being pure. In our passage in James 1:23–25 above, we see that followers of God, the set-apart ones or the congregation of Israel, are to be hearers but also doers of God's Word. This implies a partnership.

Because of our faith in Yeshua's work on the Cross, God gives us righteousness and adoption into His family. Then He asks us to be holy by being doers of His Word by studying, or looking intently, at the perfect Law and abiding in it. The underlying Hebrew word here for Law is, of course — you guessed it — *Torah*.

We are partners not in righteousness but in the work of doing the perfect Law. Righteousness comes through faith. Holiness is our part, and we show ourselves a member of the family by following God's ways.

So What Are We Saying?

Undoubtedly, some would doubt that the Bible ever instructs us to be holy. They would say that we are holy by being believers through the salvation offered by God through faith. But they mix up holiness and righteousness, don't they? Yes, all believers are righteous. We inherit that by faith. But holiness is our part, and we are admonished multiple times in His word to be so. You are probably familiar with the Old Testament admonitions to "Be holy for I am holy." You can find these instructions in Leviticus 11, 19, 20, and 21.

But there is another one as well. And the quotes from these Old Testament chapters are found in the New Testament.

> As obedient children, do not be conformed to the former lusts *which were yours* in your ignorance, but like the Holy One who called you, be holy yourselves also in all *your* behavior; because it is written, "YOU SHALL BE HOLY, FOR I AM HOLY." knowing that you were not redeemed with perishable things like silver or gold from your futile way of life inherited from your forefathers, but with precious blood, as of a lamb unblemished and spotless, *the blood* of Christ. (1 Peter 1:14–19)

God's instructions here are to not be conformed or found in obedience to our former lusts. Through wisdom and knowledge we are to modify and align our behavior to His ways. So where do we find God's ways and holiness defined? Of course — in the passages referred to above in Leviticus. In fact, the only place in God's Word where we can find His standards for holiness, for proper thinking, and for behaving on a daily basis defined, are in Torah.

Yes, in almost all of the other books in the Bible we do find references to His ways, but they all are expounding on these face-to-face communications between God and Moses at Mt. Sinai. And that is Torah.

Even the Gospels, which contain many quotes from Yeshua, only explain, help clarify, and show the applicability of the words first given to Moses. He is not giving us new laws to live by. Although He makes mention of many laws and holy principles that should guide us in our daily decision making, all of them are originally found in Torah. And to top it off, in the very last book in the Bible, God confirms that He is still being measured by these same principles of holiness.

> And the four living creatures, each one of them having six wings, are full of eyes around and within; and day and night they do not cease to say, "HOLY, HOLY, HOLY *is* THE LORD GOD, THE ALMIGHTY, WHO WAS AND WHO IS AND WHO IS TO COME." (Revelation 4:8)

This passage is quoting from Isaiah 6:3 and reveals the perpetuity of God's example of holiness for us. Should we also follow in His footsteps, and will that also be the measuring rod He will use to judge us? Or will there be another?

Once we are reunited with God and are in His presence, acting as His bride, can you imagine the conflict with Him if He were living one lifestyle and we were living a totally different lifestyle because we believed that His lifestyle had been abolished? As all married couples realize, when there are differences of morals, values, and behaviors, one of two things has to happen. Either there will be a divorce or someone will have to change.

Can you imagine a groom who would tell his bride how to be holy at the beginning of their engagement, only to nullify all of those principles at the beginning of their marriage . . . but only for her? He would then continue to live in accord with these holy principles while she would be allowed to not follow them at all . . . or some limited version.

Doesn't make a whole lot of sense, does it?

Chapter 5
Called to Be Holy

Many in the church today interpret these directives to be holy and good, and to love the Lord and love your neighbor as yourself, as a call to doing the Ten Commandments. Or, in addition, maybe it could be a call to do other kinds of good things for the people around us. Like visiting those in the hospital; or making a meal for someone who is sick; or being kind instead of exploding in anger when we are agitated. Indeed, those kindnesses are certainly signs that we are trying to be holy. But rarely do we interpret these calls for holiness as a call to live our lives by a standard such as what is defined in the Bible.

If we did we would become experts by making it a point to learn, memorize, and implement these biblical ideals. Instead, we approach God's ways in more of a whimsical, situational way, always keeping in mind how we feel. Our emotions are the determining factors in the way we think and behave. But it should not be so. God's standards are written down for us so there could be no misunderstanding. We have laws about how we can drive on the road in America. These laws are not subject to how we feel that day, or if we are late for work. They are fixed. God's laws are no different.

A Test by Fire, but for Exactly Who?

We are called to have works of holiness, and we are told that these works will be tested by fire.

> Now if any man builds on the foundation with gold, silver, precious stones, wood, hay, straw, each man's work will become evident; for the day will show it because it is *to be* revealed with fire, and the fire itself will test the quality of each man's work. If any man's work which he has built on it remains, he will receive a reward. If any man's work is burned up, he will suffer loss; but he himself will be saved, yet so as through fire. (1 Corinthians 3:12–15)

Some will have all of their works destroyed by this test. Others will not. But even those believers who have the fire destroy all their earthly works will be saved and will not suffer eternity without their Creator. This passage proves the inability of our works to bring us salvation. Only righteousness through faith can accomplish salvation.

However, this passage also establishes that the person who has no godly works will suffer loss. What, exactly, is that loss?

> I have fought the good fight, I have finished the race, I have kept the faith. [8] Now there is in store for me the crown of righteousness, which the Lord, the righteous Judge, will award to me on that day — and not only to me, but also to all who have longed for his appearing. (2 Timothy 4:7,8)

Here, Paul is stating that he has run the race and won. Certainly, he is not referring to his salvation, but rather, to a reward in addition to his salvation.

In contrast, John 3:16 states:

> For God so loved the world that he gave his one and only Son, that whoever believes in him shall not perish but have eternal life.

The word in the 2 Timothy quote above, for "crown," is *atarah* in Hebrew. This word does not mean "crown" only, but it also refers to something that is given to someone who is royal. In other words, in this case, the king's wife.

It sounds like John is suggesting that there's no "running the race" required, or "works" required, just faith and trust in God to redeem men's souls on that last day. However, Paul seems to be suggesting, in 1 Corinthians and 2 Timothy, that our works, once we are righteous, will be tested. And in order for those works to stand the test of fire, some sort of "running a race" is required. And there are rewards, in addition to salvation, that God intends to give to those who win the race.

John seems to be suggesting that faith is all that is required for salvation. There is nothing about works here. Let's see if there are other passages in the Bible, suggesting that God intends to reward works in addition to salvation.

> For the Son of Man is going to come in his Father's glory with his angels, and then he will reward each person according to what they have done. (Matthew 16:27)

The Greek word *praxis* for "what they have done" in

the passage above means "a deed, an act, or a mode of acting." The Hebrew equivalent word is *ashah,* which means, "to labor, to work upon, to make, to produce something by labor." There is not a sense at all in these words about faith, is there? They all revolve around producing something by working. What do you suppose this labor is all about?

We're also all familiar with the parable of the talents, in Matthew 25:14–29.

> And this gospel of the kingdom will be preached in the whole world as a testimony to all nations, and then the end will come. 15 "So when you see standing in the holy place 'the abomination that causes desolation,' spoken of through the prophet Daniel — let the reader understand — 16 then let those who are in Judea flee to the mountains. 17 Let no one on the housetop go down to take anything out of the house. 18 Let no one in the field go back to get their cloak. 19 How dreadful it will be in those days for pregnant women and nursing mothers! 20 Pray that your flight will not take place in winter or on the Sabbath. 21 For then there will be great distress, unequaled from the beginning of the world until now — and never to be equaled again.

> 22 "If those days had not been cut short, no one would survive, but for the sake of the elect those days will be shortened. 23 At that time if anyone says to you, 'Look, here is the

Messiah!' or, 'There he is!' do not believe it.
²⁴ For false messiahs and false prophets will
appear and perform great signs and wonders
to deceive, if possible, even the elect. ²⁵ See, I
have told you ahead of time. ²⁶ "So if anyone
tells you, 'There he is, out in the wilderness,'
do not go out; or, 'Here he is, in the inner
rooms,' do not believe it. ²⁷ For as lightning
that comes from the east is visible even in the
west, so will be the coming of the Son of Man.
²⁸ W herever there is a carcass, there the
vultures will gather. ²⁹ "Immediately after the
distress of those days "'the sun will be
darkened, and the moon will not give its
light; the stars will fall from the sky, and the
heavenly bodies will be shaken.'

Here we see servants being given varying amounts
of money, which the master expected them to invest.
Some did very well, and by working and investing
wisely produced a gain in wealth for the master.
Obviously, God is using this parable to set up his
expectations for those who come into the faith. He
wants them not only to believe and become part of
his family, but he also invests in them expecting a
gain via their work, an increase of the kingdom of
God on earth. In the parable there was one who
simply buried the money he was given. In other
words he was a servant of the most high God but
decided not to do anything with the assets entrusted
to him.

> For whoever has will be given more, and they will
> have an abundance. Whoever does not have, even

what they have will be taken from them. 30 And throw that worthless servant outside, into the darkness, where there will be weeping and gnashing of teeth.'

The servant who buried his money is called an unprofitable servant in the passage above. Is he one who ran the race but didn't win, or one who didn't even try to win? What happens to this poor soul?

Verse 30 says that this servant is thrown into outer darkness. Again we see the correlation that James also brings out, where faith is substantiated by your works. And without any works, there is no evidence that you have any faith. In other words, you can't be righteous without the proof of holiness working in your life.

What good is it, my brothers and sisters, if someone claims to have faith but has no deeds? Can such faith save them? 15 Suppose a brother or a sister is without clothes and daily food. 16 If one of you says to them, "Go in peace; keep warm and well fed," but does nothing about their physical needs, what good is it? 17 In the same way, faith by itself, if it is not accompanied by action, is dead.

18 But someone will say, "You have faith; I have deeds." Show me your faith without deeds, and I will show you my faith by my deeds. 19 You believe that there is one God. Good! Even the demons believe that — and shudder.

20 You foolish person, do you want evidence that faith without deeds is useless? 21 Was not our father Abraham considered righteous for what he did when he offered his son Isaac on the altar? 22 You see that his

faith and his actions were working together, and his faith was made complete by what he did. [23] And the scripture was fulfilled that says, "Abraham believed God, and it was credited to him as righteousness," and he was called God's friend. [24] You see that a person is considered righteous by what they do and not by faith alone.

[25] In the same way, was not even Rahab the prostitute considered righteous for what she did when she gave lodging to the spies and sent them off in a different direction? [26] As the body without the spirit is dead, so faith without deeds is dead. (James 2:14–26)

The parable of the talents follows another parable, of the wise and foolish virgins. Recall that they all had lamps. Here, the lamp metaphor explained that they all had some light in their lives, but they were scolded for not having enough light (i.e., oil) to get them through dark or difficult times. These unprepared virgins had an ending similar to that of the servant who buried his money.

"Look, I am coming soon! My reward is with me, and I will give to each person according to what they have done. (Revelation 22:12)

The above passage also talks about God coming back, with rewards for every man, not according to his faith but according to what he has actually done. Again, the Messiah is stating pretty clearly that more than faith alone is required.

So we make it our goal to please him, whether we are at home in the body or away from it. [10] For we must all appear before the judgment seat of Christ, so that each of us may receive what is due us for the things done while in the body, whether good or bad. (2 Corinthians 5:9,10)

This passage also makes the same point again. We will be recompensed for our deeds according to what we have done, whether good or bad.

Chapter 6
Our Relationship with God

Why do so many parables in the Bible make reference to grooms, groomsmen, brides, bridesmaids, and guests? Is God suggesting that, as the various parties in a wedding have different responsibilities and authorities, so too in the kingdom of God? What would you suppose that God is giving away as rewards in His kingdom? On earth a nice reward would be gold, but in the kingdom of God I believe we will walk on gold instead.

In God's eyes, the greatest reward that He could possibly give a person would be personal intimacy and proximity with Him. We see this expressed in Luke 14:8–10, below:

> "When someone invites you to a wedding feast, do not take the place of honor, for a person more distinguished than you may have been invited. 9 If so, the host who invited both of you will come and say to you, 'Give this person your seat.' Then, humiliated, you will have to take the least important place. 10 But when you are invited, take the lowest place, so that when your host comes, he will say to you, 'Friend, move up to a better place.' Then you will be honored in the presence of all the other guests. For all those who exalt themselves will be humbled, and those who humble themselves will be exalted."

This passage makes it clear that in the kingdom of God He will exalt and honor those who have served Him well by giving them a place of honor, closer to

Him. In the kingdom of God that is coming, basic authorities, responsibilities, and positions of authority will be given to those who have shown themselves to be good stewards, not with just faith and reliance on God but by doing and accomplishing the works of God here in this life.

The concept of salvation through faith is "to be called out," in this case by God. All throughout the Bible, God's people are called Israel, whether in the New or the Old Testament. These people have also been called the "called out ones," starting when Israel was "called out" from Egypt. The Hebrew word that God uses is *kehela*. In the New Testament, the Greek Septuagint equivalent for this Hebrew word is *ecklasia,* which means exactly the same thing. However, it usually gets interpreted as "church."

Unfortunately, the connectivity between the called out ones, in the Old Testament and in the New Testament, is destroyed by the different English words chosen in our English translations, even though God Himself is being very consistent. He constantly refers to His people as the ones who have been called out from among the nations.

These "called out" ones are referred to many times as sanctified. God is saying that, by being sanctified, "You are mine and I will protect you." This is what God accomplishes through our faith in Him. However, God has also required us to "set apart" ourselves from the world. This "setting apart" is accomplished by our works of obedience to His ways, His principles, and His directions for our lives.

The concept of Hebrew betrothal carries this same idea with it. During the betrothal period, equivalent in our day to the engagement period, people realize that they need to set themselves apart for their bride or groom. In other words, they stop doing certain types of behaviors, such as ogling others of the opposite sex and perhaps thinking inappropriate thoughts about others. Certainly they cease from dating others.

Rather, engaged people begin to focus all their attention, all their love, and all their hopes and dreams on their intended spouse. In this way they are set apart for their beloved. As we also are engaged to our Messiah (Groom), should we be conforming our ways to His will? His reward, his recognition of our loyalty, may very much be determined by what we do per His Word rather than just our faith alone.

Exodus 19:5 tells us:

> Now therefore, if ye will obey my voice indeed, and keep my covenant, then ye shall be a peculiar treasure unto me above all people: for all the earth is mine.

In this passage God calls His people a "peculiar treasure." However, in order for us to actually be treasured by God, this verse proposes nothing about faith. It talks about qualifications to be treasured by God, via obedience, and by keeping His covenant, which is a reference to His commandments. Recall that the book of covenant is what God called "Torah," and in the Bible, Torah as interpreted as "the Laws of God."

Is God proposing here that, in order to please Him, we simply have to obey His Laws? And, that doing so is proof to Him of our faith? Again, this echoes the concept expressed in James, that faith is worthless without any evidence of it, without any works of obedience.

This intimacy is made clear in Matthew 7:21–23:

> "Not everyone who says to me, 'Lord, Lord,' will enter the kingdom of heaven, but only the one who does the will of my Father who is in heaven. 22 Many will say to me on that day, 'Lord, Lord, did we not prophesy in your name and in your name drive out demons and in your name perform many miracles?' 23 Then I will tell them plainly, 'I never knew you. Away from me, you evildoers!'

God suggests that there will be people who actually performed miracles in their lifetimes on earth, but God will also say that they were evildoers and that He never knew them. The Hebrew word here, for "knew," is *Yada*. It means, "to know" as in "to know information," but also it's the word used in the Old Testament to describe the "knowing" a couple would have that produced offspring.

Obviously, this is a reference to the very intimate sexual act between married couples that produces children. What God is proposing, by using this word here, is that maybe He "knew of them" but He never "knew" them as friends and spouses know each other. They never invested the time to get to know their Creator; their works did not survive the test of fire and neither did their faith.

In the Christian church today there is a common belief that we should be "good" once we are saved. But how is this goodness defined? Does God define it, or is it something subjectively discerned by us on a moment-by-moment basis? I think we have learned, in the passages above, that God has clearly delineated that definition. It is not subject to our feelings or whims, and it certainly is not subjective. Rather, it is a standard created by God and established and reiterated multiple times in His Word. For that reason alone this standard should be learned and memorized and then observed throughout our lives.

The circumstances that come up in our daily lives should be measured by this fixed standard. The decisions we make should not be governed by our feelings, but rather by His fixed standard. And in so doing, we create "works" in our lives that will stand the test of fire. We become holy to God and a peculiar treasure to Him.

The Greatest Commandment

"Teacher, which is the greatest commandment in the Law?" [37] Jesus replied: "'Love the Lord your God with all your heart and with all your soul and with all your mind.' [38] This is the first and greatest commandment. [39] And the second is like it: 'Love your neighbor as yourself.' ⁴⁰ All the Law and the Prophets hang on these two commandments." (Matthew 22:36–40

These are the commands, decrees and laws the LORD your God directed me to teach you to observe in the land that you are crossing the Jordan to possess, ² so that you, your children and their children after them may fear the LORD your God as long as you live by keeping all his decrees and commands that I give you, and so that you may enjoy long life. ³ Hear, Israel, and be careful to obey so that it may go well with you and that you may increase greatly in a land flowing with milk and honey, just as the LORD, the God of your ancestors, promised you. ⁴ Hear, O Israel: The LORD our God, the LORD is one. ⁵ Love the LORD your God with all your heart and with all your soul and with all your strength. ⁶ These commandments that I give you today are to be on your hearts. ⁷ Impress them on your children. Talk about them when you sit at home and when you walk along the road, when you lie down and when you get up. ⁸ Tie them as symbols on your hands and bind them on your foreheads. ⁹ Write them on the doorframes of your houses and on your gates. (Deuteronomy 6:1–9)

But the land you are crossing the Jordan to take possession of is a land of mountains and valleys that drinks rain from heaven. ¹² It is a land the LORD your God cares for; the eyes of the LORD your God are continually on it from the beginning of the year to its end. ¹³ So if you faithfully obey the commands I am giving you today — to love the LORD your God and to serve him with all your heart and with all your soul — ¹⁴ then I will send rain on your land in its season, both autumn and spring rains, so that you may gather in your grain, new wine and olive oil. (Deuteronomy 11:11–14)

For I command you today to love the LORD your God, to walk in obedience to him, and to keep his

> commands, decrees and laws; then you will live and increase, and the LORD your God will bless you in the land you are entering to possess. (Deuteronomy 30:16)

In our passage from Matthew 22, Yeshua is asked about which is the greatest command. His answer is very interesting, and should be especially so for those who believe that the "Law" has been abolished. In His answer he implied nothing of the kind. In fact, He grouped the Law into two broad categories.

The first group included all those Laws that, if obeyed, would elevate God to a position of honor and worship in our lives. The second group of Laws were all those that, if obeyed, would elevate our neighbor to the next most important position of honor in our lives. In this way Yeshua made it clear that by obedience to the Law we would honor and elevate our God and our neighbor. Nowhere does He suggest that we can accomplish the same by any other means.

Matthew 22:37, above, is quoting from multiple places in the Old Testament, some of which we've also included above. In these passages, God links loving Him with keeping His commandments. He also links loving and keeping His commandments with earning a blessing. This echoes, of course, the New Testament passage that says:

> If you love me, keep my commandments. [21] Whoever has my commands and keeps them is the one who loves me. The one who loves me will be loved by my Father, and I too will love them and show myself to them." (John 14:15,21)

Here, John is echoing the Old Testament concepts, supporting the idea, again, that God's Word presents one panoramic view of His workings with man, and how He wants man to honor and obey Him. One way, a set of Laws, did not get abolished and replaced by another way.

And remember, for those who believe that, upon Yeshua's death and resurrection the Law was then put aside (i.e., "hung on the cross"), John wrote his verses post-resurrection. The Law had the same standing before as well as after, supporting the idea that the purpose of Yeshua's life and His work had nothing to do with abolishing anything. The only thing the work of Yeshua's life abolished was the incorrect understanding and error in His people's belief about His Word, and how that Word should be applied to their lives. Thus the idea of abolishing the Law is a very clumsy interpretation, especially when you are using Yeshua's own words.

In Matthew 5:17–19, Yeshua makes the reason for His coming very clear. He specifically states that He did not come to abolish the Law, but that He came to fulfill it. In Greek, the word for "fulfill" means to "fill up, to make full, to abound, to liberally supply." The Hebrew equivalent word here is *mala*, which means "to be full, to fill up even to overflowing."

> "Do not think that I have come to abolish the Law or the Prophets; I have not come to abolish them but to fulfill them. [18] For truly I tell you, until heaven and earth disappear, not the smallest letter, not the least stroke of a pen, will by any means disappear from the Law until everything is accomplished. [19] Therefore anyone who sets aside one of the least of these commands and teaches others accordingly will be called least in the kingdom of heaven, but whoever practices and teaches these commands will be called great in the kingdom of heaven. (Matthew 5:17–19)

A related Hebrew word is *malach*, which means "salt." Recall that God's called-out ones, and those that have set themselves apart, are to be "salt" to the world. What are the qualities of salt? First of all, it adds flavor to food. It is also a preservative and can protect food from decay. This is exactly what the works of holiness are supposed to do — the works that will stand the test of fire. They are supposed to add flavor to the lives around us, and also to be a preservative by standing against sin, which we all know causes decay and death.

But assuming that everyone wants to have something to offer to God that will earn them a reward, just what are we called to do? As we have learned, it is what we do according to His will that will count. The primary thing God has called us all *to be* and *to do* is to *be holy*. But are there different standards today depending on whether you are a Jew or a Gentile?

Some say yes. However, is God saying that there are two standards for holiness that we will be judged by? Did Yeshua come and die for the sins of the Jews that are different than the sins of the Gentiles? Are there multiple sets of laws applicable to different races of people? Or is there only grace, and no standard to worry about at all?

Do we become righteous and holy as soon as we become believers? Most of us would agree from our study so far that this is not very likely. We are called to live by a standard that will create holiness, or works, that will stand the test by fire. And there is righteousness that we inherit through faith.

But what about the other questions? Let us now explore some of the alternatives to what I believe God is saying to us in His Word. Is there one Law for all, and all for one, or are the Jews and the Gentiles given different standards by which God will measure their lives? In other words, did Yeshua come and die for the sins of Israel that were different than the sin of the Gentiles?

These questions are big issues today, and they generate a lot of different opinions. The Christian world, for the most part, teaches that Christian believers are responsible to keep most of the Ten Commandments, along with a vague and variable list of do's and don'ts. As far as the other Laws are concerned, as found in the Old Testament, they believe that those commands from God have mostly been abolished.

We will discuss this further later on in our study, but I bring this up now because the Christian church believes in two sets of Laws. One set has been abolished and another is mostly defined by the Ten Commandments. Meanwhile, the Jews also propose two sets of Laws: One applicable to the Gentiles and one applicable to themselves.

Chapter 7
Believers: The First Group

In these two final chapters we would like to review what we have stated already in the context of what we are obligated to do to be holy. Yes, there is a difference between holiness and righteousness. Righteousness we get for free. We are given this Godly quality via our faith and reliance on the work of Yeshua's death on the Cross. His sacrifice paid the price for our sin, and we can receive restoration back to our Maker by accepting this free gift of salvation.

On the other hand, we have learned that holiness is something different altogether. This is our part of the relationship. God has called us to be holy, to live our lives according to His principles. He calls these Laws holy in His Word, and conformity to these Laws brings holiness to us as we line up our lives to them. We do not become righteous by obeying them; we become holy.

Now let's explore exactly what part of the Laws of God are still applicable. Knowing that the application of these Laws will bring a transformation of our lives from unholy to holy, we should be very interested in becoming aware of our obligation to usher in this transformation in conformity to God's directives.

In our future writings we will deal with the subject of exactly what the Law is, and what is still applicable to mankind today, in a much more thorough way. However, we feel that it would be appropriate to spend a bit of time here to make some small points about the Law's applicability. If we are truly interested in being holy, then this issue is of paramount importance and justifies, at the very least, a basic review right here.

Two groups of interested parties come to mind when we consider the applicability of the Laws of God.

- Over the centuries, the Christian church and its adherents and teachers have taken many positions concerning that subject. Christians would certainly be one of these groups.

- The other group would include the Torah-believing Jews and the Messianic believers in the Messiah of the Tanach and the Brit Hadashah (the Old and the New Testaments).

I have lumped the Torah-believing Jews and the Messianic believers together, in the second group, because they tend to have somewhat similar positions concerning the Law. Also, they both believe in the Messiah but differ on whether Yeshua (Jesus) was in fact the fulfillment of the messianic prophecies. Let's address that group first.

Noahide Laws: Are the Rabbis Correct?

The Jews mostly teach that in order for them to have a place in the world to come they need to keep all of the 613 Laws that they have identified in Torah. This group of Laws is called the *mitzvoth*. They believe that these Laws were issued to the Jews only, and are therefore binding only upon themselves, having inherited the obligation from their ancestors.

Many members of Messianic congregations also believe essentially the same thing. Their ideas have been called the Doctrine of Two Laws. More about that to come. But for now, many in the Jewish as well as the Messianic congregations believe that there is one set of Laws for the Jew and one set of Laws for the Gentile.

Many in these two subgroups above believe that the Gentiles should just keep the set of Laws that are called the Noahide Laws. This list includes the following:

> No idolatry
> No murder
> No theft
> No sexual immorality
> No blasphemy
> No eating flesh taken from an animal while it is still alive
> You shall establish a set of courts of Law

The rabbis created this list around the year 200 AD. According to the Talmud (a Jewish commentary on the Torah), the Noahide Laws were given by God as a binding set of Laws for the "children of Noah," which is a Jewish reference to all of mankind. Any non-Jew who adheres to these Laws is regarded as a righteous Gentile and is assured of a place in the world to come.

Now of course, as we have already pointed out, salvation does not come by works but by faith. However, our point here is to delineate what different positions others have concerning the Law. This opinion is certainly the Jews' majority position, but other rabbis disagree. Some believe that the Gentiles are even forbidden to obey any of the other Laws in Torah beyond the Noahide Laws. Some suppose that the rabbis came up with this short list for the Gentiles as a result of thinking that the Jews were special or more important in God's eyes.

Whatever their motive, most Christian believers are probably just thankful that the Jewish rabbis' belief corroborates their own pastors' teachings that the Gentiles are not required to obey most of the ordinances found in the Old Testament. These would include dietary Laws, honoring Shabbat, and celebrating the feasts of God.

But where did this list of seven Laws come from? Can we support these ideas with the biblical text?

> "Only you shall not eat flesh with its life, *that is,* its blood. Surely I will require your lifeblood; from every beast I will require it. And from *every* man, from every man's brother I will require the life of man. "Whoever

> sheds man's blood, by man his blood shall be shed, for in the image of God He made man. (Genesis 9:4–6)

In this passage, God is changing what is food for man. Before the flood, God instructed Adam that only the plants were given for food.

> Then God said, "Behold, I have given you every plant yielding seed that is on the surface of all the earth, and every tree which has fruit yielding seed; it shall be food for you; and to every beast of the earth and to every bird of the sky and to everything that moves on the earth which has life, *I have given* every green plant for food"; and it was so. (Genesis 1:29, 30)

Evidently mankind, as well as all the animals, were given only plants for food. Everything that had life, everything that breathed, was to eat only plants. And this included mankind. But after the flood God expanded the definition of what could be considered food, to include animals. But He is giving mankind some guidelines in doing so. The meat must not contain blood. It should be drained out before we can eat it.

Also, here in this biblical text we find another of the Noahide Laws listed above: Do not murder another person. So far so good. We have support for two of these Laws. The rabbis draw from Genesis chapter two to support the balance of the list of seven.

> The LORD God commanded the man, saying, "From any tree of the garden you may eat freely; (Genesis 2:16)

They use verse 16 to support the other five Noahide Laws. However, after reading this verse I was a bit confused because I couldn't find any reference to the other Laws. The word for 'commanded' didn't help. It just means "to command or appoint." But there was nothing there that referred to any Laws specifically, or implied a list of do's and don'ts.

The only possible conclusion was that this list was made up. Oh, certainly one can find all of these seven Laws in the Bible, but they were not created by God as a specific list such as we find when we read the Ten Commandments. Nor did God ever direct the Gentiles to obey these Noahide Laws. And for that matter, nor did He ever direct the Gentiles to obey only the list we know as the Ten Commandments.

Was Mankind Truly Given Two Sets of Laws?

But what about the exclusivity of the Law? Was the Law given for only the Jews to obey, thus allowing non-Jews to be responsible to God differently? In other words, did God create two ways to be holy during ancient times, before the coming of Yeshua?

This question is somewhat involved, but the short answer is no. God did not create two sets of Laws. His Law's applicability was never put in the context of race. Let's take a closer look to see.

> 'There shall be one standard for you; it shall be for the stranger as well as the native, for I am the LORD your God.'" (Leviticus 24:22)

Before we can properly understand this passage we need to review the composition of the congregation of Israel. We are very familiar with the confusion that occurred after Yeshua rose from the dead. As Paul went out to introduce the risen Savior to the Gentiles, a huge question and a huge dispute arose among all of the believers. What part of the Law was applicable to these new converts? Should they be responsible to obey all of the Law? Or, as many believe today, does grace now abound, thus abolishing the need to conform to these Laws?

This same question came up as Moses attempted to make these Laws part of Israel's everyday life. Most of us believe that the people who walked through the Red Sea and then walked about in the Wilderness those forty years constituted the sons and daughters of the twelve sons of Israel. But is that correct?

Here we have a pronouncement that there should be one Law, or one standard, for the stranger as well as the native-born. The reference to the "stranger" refers to a Gentile who is now a follower/believer of the God of Israel. This verse, and many others by the way, implies that there were many people who were not Jewish in the camp of Israel.

> Now the sons of Israel journeyed from Rameses to Succoth, about six hundred thousand men on foot, aside from children. [38]A mixed multitude also went up

> with them, along with flocks and herds, a very large
> number of livestock. (Exodus 12:38)

The Hebrew word for "mixed multitude" is *arev*, which means "strangers, aliens," specifically not descendants of the sons of Israel.

Here we see that there were many other races that also came out of the captivity of Egypt along with the sons of Israel. These races intermixed with the sons of Israel over time, and became indistinguishable from the Hebrews with respect to which of the twelve tribes they belonged. We see an example of this when Moses sent the twelve spies into the Promised Land.

> 'None of the men who came up from Egypt, from
> twenty years old and upward, shall see the land which
> I swore to Abraham, to Isaac and to Jacob; for they did
> not follow Me fully, 12 except Caleb the son of
> Jephunneh the Kenizzite and Joshua the son of Nun,
> for they have followed the LORD fully.' 13 So the LORD'S
> anger burned against Israel, and He made them
> wander in the wilderness forty years, until the entire
> generation of those who had done evil in the sight of
> the LORD was destroyed. (Numbers 32:11–13)

This passage informs us that Caleb, one of the twelve spies, was a Kenizzite. Gesenius informs us that the Kenizzites were a Canaanite nation of people. They were descendants of Canaan, the son of Ham, whereas the Hebrews were descendants of Shem, Ham's brother. However, in the list of the names of the twelve spies who were chosen to go into the Promised Land, we discover that Caleb is referred to as from the tribe of Judah.

> . . . from the tribe of Judah, Caleb the son of
> Jephunneh . . . (Numbers 13:6)

In other words, the person who was selected to represent the tribe of Judah in the spies that were sent into the Promised Land had a lineage that was not from Shem, but from Ham. Certainly all the descendants of Ham would be described as aliens, Gentiles, or foreigners and were certainly not from the tribe of Judah. But here we see that Caleb had become one with the sons of Israel yet *was not a literal descendent of Israel.*

Throughout the Bible we see this same phenomenon in which the nation of Israel is referred to as the descendants of Jacob, but they also include other races as well. Could it be true that the descendants of Jacob, the ones God called out from among the nations to be His people, are continually being expanded by other races joining in with them?

Here is what the Apostle Paul had to say:

> I am telling the truth in Christ, I am not lying, my conscience testifies with me in the Holy Spirit, 2 that I have great sorrow and unceasing grief in my heart. 3 For I could wish that I myself were accursed, *separated* from Christ for the sake of my brethren, my kinsmen according to the flesh, 4 who are Israelites, to whom belongs the adoption as sons, and the glory and the covenants and the giving of the Law and the *temple* service and the promises, 5 whose are the fathers, and from whom is the Christ according to the flesh, who is over all, God blessed forever. Amen.

⁶ But *it is* not as though the word of God has failed. For they are not all Israel who are *descended* from Israel; ⁷ nor are they all children because they are Abraham's descendants, but: "THROUGH ISAAC YOUR DESCENDANTS WILL BE NAMED." ⁸ That is, it is not the children of the flesh who are children of God, but the children of the promise are regarded as descendants. ⁹ For this is the word of promise: "AT THIS TIME I WILL COME, AND SARAH SHALL HAVE A SON." ¹⁰ And not only this, but there was Rebekah also, when she had conceived *twins* by one man, our father Isaac; ¹¹ for though *the twins* were not yet born and had not done anything good or bad, so that God's purpose according to *His* choice would stand, not because of works but because of Him who calls, ¹² it was said to her, "THE OLDER WILL SERVE THE YOUNGER." ¹³ Just as it is written, "JACOB I LOVED, BUT ESAU I HATED."

¹⁴ What shall we say then? There is no injustice with God, is there? May it never be! ¹⁵ For He says to Moses, "I WILL HAVE MERCY ON WHOM I HAVE MERCY, AND I WILL HAVE COMPASSION ON WHOM I HAVE COMPASSION." ¹⁶ So then it *does* not *depend* on the man who wills or the man who runs, but on God who has mercy. ¹⁷ For the Scripture says to Pharaoh, "FOR THIS VERY PURPOSE I RAISED YOU UP, TO DEMONSTRATE MY POWER IN YOU, AND THAT MY NAME MIGHT BE PROCLAIMED THROUGHOUT THE WHOLE EARTH." ¹⁸ So then He has mercy on whom He desires, and He hardens whom He desires.

¹⁹ You will say to me then, "Why does He still find fault? For who resists His will?" ²⁰ On the contrary, who are you, O man, who answers back to God? The thing molded will not say to the molder, "Why did you make me like this," will it? ²¹ Or does not the potter have a right over the clay, to make from the same lump one vessel for honorable use and another for common use? ²² What if God, although willing to demonstrate His wrath and to make His power known, endured with much patience vessels of wrath prepared for destruction? ²³ And *He did so* to make known the

riches of His glory upon vessels of mercy, which He prepared beforehand for glory, 24 *even* us, whom He also called, not from among Jews only, but also from among Gentiles.
(Romans 9:1–24)

In this passage we see that Paul refers to the literal descendants of Jacob (Israel), but he also refers to the children of the promise who are *also* regarded as descendants (verse 9). Later in verse 24 we see that God has prepared both the Jews and the Gentiles to be included in the children of promise; i.e., the descendants of Israel.

'There shall be one standard for you; it shall be for the stranger as well as the native, for I am the LORD your God.'" (Leviticus 24:22)

So, going back to our verse above, God is making it clear here that, whether you are a literal son of Israel or a stranger, the Law applies to you. There are many other verses that say the same thing. However, let's take a closer look at this passage.

The Hebrew word here for "stranger" is *gar*. This word gets translated as "stranger, alien, and sojourner," but in this passage it is referring to a person who is not a physical descendant of Israel but has taken upon himself the same belief in the one true God. We learn here that this person is required to follow the same Law or standard as the native born. The word "native" in our verse above refers to people who are identified as physical descendants of Israel. Both of these peoples are responsible to live according to the "standard." The

Hebrew word for "standard" here is *mishpat*. This is a very commonly used word to describe the divine Laws of God as given to Moses on Mt Sinai.

So, there seems to be a problem here with what some Jewish Rabbis teach, and what some Messianic believers believe, with respect to the exclusivity of the Law, which they teach (and believe) only applies to the Jews. We believe that the Law was given to Israel, and "Israel" is a word used to describe the descendants of Jacob, but it also included those people from other races who take on the same belief of the one true God as revealed in the Tanach.

In both the Jewish and Messianic communities we find a common belief that disagrees with our points above. Their ideas are known by some as the "Two-Law Doctrine." This belief claims that God has given one Law to the Jews and another Law to the Gentiles. Thus, they claim that there are two Laws to be followed, one by each group for salvation with respect to the Jewish Rabbi's belief, or for holiness with respect to the messianic Rabbi's position.

Obviously, that idea is not new and has been proposed by many throughout the ages. But can we find where God's Law is differentiated by race? If so, what portion of the Law would be applicable to the person who is only half-Jewish or some other percentage, smaller or greater? Would only half of the principles of holiness apply to him? If so, I wonder if he would be able to pick which half of the Law he wanted to conform to.

Of course that's ridiculous. Here in the modern age it is very likely that no one knows beyond a shadow of doubt their exact lineage. Therefore, no Jew can claim for certainty that they are 100% a descendant of Israel, and no Gentile can claim that they have no Israelite blood flowing through their veins. Thus the argument that one is of Jewish or Gentile descent, and therefore that one of these sets of Laws is or is not applicable, would be unknowable if the two-Law position were actually true.

The question then arises: Would God create such a system, whereby after many generations, mankind would not be able to know which of the two sets of Laws was applicable to him? I don't think so. My point again is that there is one Law and it is applicable to both Jews and Gentiles; i.e., all those who love the creator God who calls himself *Yahowah,* as spelled *yod, hey, vav, hey.* And furthermore, those people whom the Bible calls *Israel* must trust and rely on the promises of God to save and cleanse their souls through the work on the cross of the Messiah two thousand years ago.

Chapter 8
Believers: The Second Group

But what about the Christians, many of whom believe that the Law has been abolished and give the Old Testament Laws no heed whatsoever. Usually, those in the church today do follow the Ten Commandments, except for the fourth commandment that tells us to rest on the Sabbath, which should also be Saturday rather than Sunday.

Some also follow some vague general group of ideas that help them guide their decisions throughout life. But this list differs from person-to-person and from church-to-church. There is no uniformity to the rules beyond the Ten Commandments, minus one.

Is their position justified? I suspect not. But can we challenge their doctrine concerning the applicability of the Old Testament Laws? Yes, I think we can. Certainly we can give a lot of food for thought to help get Christians thinking about these things. Remember, whether we are Jew or Gentile, we are called to be holy, "for He is holy." So for Christians the issue should be really important, especially if we have assumed that the Laws that make us holy, when we obey them, have somehow been abolished. Let's see if we can challenge these ideas at a foundational level.

I am aware that many in the church will use various passages from the writings of Paul to support their notion that the Laws have been abolished. My contention is that many of these verses are taken out of context and then used inappropriately to support ideas that Paul is not promoting. So let's see if we can get to the foundation of Paul's belief with respect to the Laws of the Old Testament in the writings of the New Testament, starting with the following passage:

> After he had greeted them, he *began* to relate one by one the things which God had done among the Gentiles through his ministry. [20] And when they heard it they *began* glorifying God; and they said to him, "You see, brother, how many thousands there are among the Jews of those who have believed, and they are all zealous for the Law; [21] and they have been told about you, that you are teaching all the Jews who are among the Gentiles to forsake Moses, telling them not to circumcise their children nor to walk according to the customs. [22] What, then, is *to be done*? They will certainly hear that you have come. [23] Therefore do this that we tell you. We have four men who are under a vow; [24] take them and purify yourself along with them, and pay their expenses so that they may shave their heads; and all will know that there is nothing to the things which they have been told about you, but that you yourself also walk orderly, keeping the Law. (Acts 21:19–24)

In this passage we hear that the Jews in Jerusalem, during this time, are all zealous for the Law. Keep in mind that this history in the book of Acts is focusing on the times that follow the death and resurrection of Yeshua/Jesus. My first question is, if Yeshua taught that the Law was going to be abolished following His resurrection, why are all the elders of the brethren, such as James — His own brother no less — and the thousands of Jews living in Jerusalem, following the Law? Did they get something wrong? Of course not.

But we will hold off a bit on what the teachings of Yeshua reveal about the Law. For now let's focus on what Paul says and does concerning the accusation in verse 21, above. He is being accused of the very same thing that the church today claims he is doing: that is, teaching others to forsake the Law. In other words he is accused here, as the church has claimed, that Paul taught that the Law had been abolished.

However, the passage above makes it clear that Paul had not forsaken the Law and that he was not teaching that others should forsake it too. In fact, in the verses that follow our quote above, to prove that he has not forsaken the Law, Paul enters into a Nazarite vow and pays the expenses of four other men who are taking the vow as well.

This is no small vow, by the way. Look it up. You can find the requirements in Numbers 6. This vow includes abstaining from wine or other strong drink, abstaining from food that contains vinegar (which, by the way, includes many foods in our diet today) or grape juice, or eating raisins. This person shall not cut the hair on their head, along with other restrictions as well.

Usually this vow would last for a lifetime, but it could also be as short as one to three years. Paul was making a very big statement by taking this vow: it was a huge price to pay to help validate his claim of not forsaking the Law and not teaching others to do so as well.

This was Paul's golden opportunity. If he actually meant to teach others to forsake the Law, why not just go ahead and confront the issue now? If he was not being truthful (which of course is ridiculous), why do we trust the teachings of Paul? How do we know when he is being truthful and when he is not? If a person believes that Paul wasn't being truthful and just sidestepping the issue, then we really need to throw out all of his writings, don't we?

The point is that he was not forsaking the Law as was the rumor of the day. Continue reading the next few chapters in Acts. In these passages, the historical record makes it clear that Paul was a follower, not a forsaker, of the Laws of God.

> But this I (Paul) admit to you, that according to the Way which they call a sect I do serve the God of our fathers, believing everything that is in accordance with the Law and that is written in the Prophets 15having a hope in God, which these men cherish themselves, that there shall certainly be a resurrection of both the righteous and the wicked. (Acts 24:14, 15)

The verses above make clear this point. So, can we logically conclude that Paul was observant of the Law and taught others to do so as well? These passages seem to be in conflict with other verses in his letters. But keep in mind, Acts is recorded history about actual events that occurred in the life of the sect of the Nazarenes in Israel, what the Christians call the "early church." We see here that these historical writings quote Paul as claiming that he is in support of the Law, that he has followed them personally all of his life, and that he is teaching others to do so as well.

Thus, this is the foundational position that students of the letters of Paul should carry in their minds as they try to understand Paul's other teachings. These writings cannot be in conflict; they must be consistent. My claim is that Paul is being truthful, here in Acts, about his behavior and teachings. All of his other writings that sometimes appear to be in conflict are, in fact, only in conflict when taken out of their contexts. Paul is also very clear in his other writings about his true opinion concerning the Laws of God.

> Do we then nullify the Law through faith? May it never be! On the contrary, we establish the Law. (Romans 3:31)

> So then, the Law is holy, and the commandment is holy and righteous and good. (Romans 7:12)

> But if I do the very thing I do not want *to do*, I agree with the Law, *confessing* that the Law is good. (Romans 7:16)

> But we know that the Law is good, if one uses it lawfully. (1 Timothy 1:8)

Thus we see that Paul also wrote supporting his foundational position regarding the Laws in Acts, and in many other places in his letters. The passages above constitute no more than a small sample of the points he makes in support of the applicability of the Law.

Now let's move on to one other passage that seems to come up regularly among Christians when discussing the relevance of the Law. This passage is Acts 15. Here we see Paul and Barnabas attending a meeting of the elders in Jerusalem to discuss issues about the Law. Many today believe that this chapter is talking about what Laws the Gentiles will be required to obey once they are saved. However, this is not the topic at all. The very first verse of chapter 15 tells us what the issue to be discussed and decided upon was:

> Some men came down from Judea and *began* teaching the brethren, "Unless you are circumcised according to the custom of Moses, you cannot be saved." (Acts 15:1)

This chapter, and the meeting of the elders, was all about which of the Laws of Moses Gentiles must observe to be SAVED. It is not about what part of the Laws of Moses are still required for Gentiles to obey, or which are applicable for the Jews, or which ones apply to anyone else for that matter. The argument and subsequent meeting was to discuss the issue of a teaching that promoted the idea that unless you are circumcised according to the customs of Moses you cannot be saved.

We could spend more time winnowing out all of the other implications of the conclusion of this counsel, but it is not really applicable to our discussion here. This meeting was for the purpose of deciding which of the Laws was pertinent for the brethren, Jew and Gentile alike, to obey for *salvation*, not *holiness*. In other words, the counsel made some conclusions about salvation and certain expectations about the behavior of someone who wanted this salvation.

Now read this chapter in Acts with that as the focus. You will gain insight into the idea that God expects at least some evidence of your faith, which gains the person righteousness or salvation.

Likewise, read what James himself said in the second chapter of his own book:

> What use is it, my brethren, if someone says he has faith but he has no works? Can that faith save him? [15] If a brother or sister is without clothing and in need of daily food, [16] and one of you says to them, "Go in peace, be warmed and be filled," and yet you do not give them what is necessary for *their* body, what use is that? [17] Even so faith, if it has no works, is dead, *being* by itself.

> [18] But someone may *well* say, "You have faith and I have works; show me your faith without the works, and I will show you my faith by my works." [19] You believe that God is one. You do well; the demons also believe, and shudder. [20] But are you willing to recognize, you foolish fellow, that faith without works is useless? [21] Was not Abraham our father justified by works when he offered up Isaac his son on the altar? [22] You see that faith was working with his works, and as a result of the works, faith was perfected; [23] and the Scripture was fulfilled which says, "AND ABRAHAM BELIEVED GOD, AND IT WAS RECKONED TO HIM AS

RIGHTEOUSNESS," and he was called the friend of God. [24] You see that a man is justified by works and not by faith alone. [25] In the same way, was not Rahab the harlot also justified by works when she received the messengers and sent them out by another way? [26] For just as the body without *the* spirit is dead, so also faith without works is dead.
(James 2:14–26)

According to James, this evidence is defined as deeds and works. And if you read this entire chapter you discover that these "deeds and works" encompass the Laws of God.

In other words, to help "bring this together," the counsel in Acts decided which of these Laws were the minimum required to justify the person's faith, thus making a person's faith come alive and be active. Of course, the implications are that there are many more Laws to be incorporated into the new believer's life, but the counsel was giving us a good starting point.

What Did Yeshua Himself Have to Say?

All of this is well and good, but we have yet to support our position that the Law is still active and its application leads to holiness by using the very words of Yeshua/Jesus. Are there such passages?

Let's take a look at Matthew chapter 5. Starting with verse 17, this passage is very pertinent to our discussion. Here Yeshua says the following:

"Do not think that I came to abolish the Law or the Prophets; I did not come to abolish but to fulfill. [18] For

> truly I say to you, until heaven and earth pass away,
> not the smallest letter or stroke shall pass from the
> Law until all is accomplished. [19] Whoever then annuls
> one of the least of these commandments, and teaches
> others *to do* the same, shall be called least in the
> kingdom of heaven; but whoever keeps and teaches
> *them*, he shall be called great in the kingdom of
> heaven. (Matthew 5:17–19)

Here we have a statement by God Himself that
claims that He has not come to abolish the Law but
He has come to fulfill it. Here the word for "fulfill" in
Greek means "to make full, to fill up, to fill to the
top, to the very brim." The Hebrew equivalent word,
maleh, means pretty much the same thing. It would
add the idea of "filling up to overflowing."

Some people suggest that the Messiah came to
abolish the Law, and they use this passage and this
word for "fulfill" to mean "complete, finish and
terminate or end the Law." In other words, "abolish
the Law" is how they want to interpret this word.

First, that is not what the word in Hebrew or Greek
means. And second, the verse would make no sense
if that were the proper understanding of this word
for "fulfill." The verse would then read, "Do not
think that I came to abolish the Law or the
Prophets; I did not come to abolish but to abolish."

Of course this is ridiculous. What Yeshua is saying is
that He did not come to *misinterpret* the Law but to
*properly explain the Law so that it would fill up our
lives and overflow to the world.* Remember, if by
doing the Law one gains holiness, Yeshua's purpose

was for us to gain a better understanding of His Law so that our holiness and light would spread throughout the world and would bless others with the realization of God's truth and holiness as well.

The point is made even clearer by the verses that follow. God makes it clear that not the smallest letter or even a single stroke shall pass from the Law until all is accomplished. And this happens when heaven and earth pass away. Well, I believe we can all testify that the earth and the heavens are still here. Thus, the Law and its applicability are also *still here*.

Yeshua goes on to warn those who want to annul even one of the least of these commandments, and teaches others to do the same, will be punished by being called the least in the kingdom of heaven. He will also reward those who keep the Law and teach others to obey it. God will reward those by calling them great in the kingdom of heaven. Pretty clear, eh?

I think a fair conclusion from the above passages is that there may be a problem with the doctrinal position that there are two Laws, one for the Jews to obey and one for everyone else. Also, the Christians may have a problem with their position that the Law has been done away with — hung on the Cross as some propose. These passages shine a clear light on the subject and should cause people to think a bit more about how they can please God by including more of His Laws into their lifestyle.

Conclusion

In closing, I would like to link together all that we have proposed here. These ideas lead to many conclusions, but one seems particularly interesting.

> "When your son asks you in time to come, saying, 'What *do* the testimonies and the statutes and the judgments *mean* which the LORD our God commanded you?' [21] then you shall say to your son, 'We were slaves to Pharaoh in Egypt, and the LORD brought us from Egypt with a mighty hand. [22] Moreover, the LORD showed great and distressing signs and wonders before our eyes against Egypt, Pharaoh and all his household; [23] He brought us out from there in order to bring us in, to give us the land which He had sworn to our fathers.' [24] So the LORD commanded us to observe all these statutes, to fear the LORD our God for our good always and for our survival, as *it is* today. [25] It will be righteousness for us if we are careful to observe all these commandments before the LORD our God, just as He commanded us. (Deuteronomy 6:20–25)

Here, God is offering a covenant with Israel that would earn them righteousness via their obedience, or work, according to the Laws of God. We will call this covenant the Sinai Covenant.

This passage seems to be saying that, if you are careful to obey all the Laws of God, you will inherit righteousness. And, in fact, that is exactly what is being offering. This is not a contradiction to the thesis of this book. It may seem ridiculous to propose, but recall that there are two ways to be in good standing/righteous/saved with God. Adam and

Eve were righteous, in good standing with God. They had eternal salvation and life before they sinned. And so can we if we are able to live a perfect life.

However, Yeshua is the only one who has ever procured righteousness via this Sinai Covenant. He certainly didn't procure His righteousness via faith.

Now, we all realize that obedience to the Sinai Covenant is impossible except for Him. But God put forth this way of becoming righteous here in our passage above, so that His Son could qualify for righteousness under this Sinai Covenant, thereby giving Him the ability to pay the price for our sins through the shedding of His blood.

The Israelites were even asked to enter into this Sinai Covenant in an effort to also receive this blessing of righteousness.

> He sent young men of the sons of Israel, and they offered burnt offerings and sacrificed young bulls as peace offerings to the LORD. [6] Moses took half of the blood and put *it* in basins, and the *other* half of the blood he sprinkled on the altar. [7] Then he took the book of the covenant and read *it* in the hearing of the people; and they said, "All that the LORD has spoken we will do, and we will be obedient!" [8] So Moses took the blood and sprinkled *it* on the people, and said, "Behold the blood of the covenant, which the LORD has made with you in accordance with all these words." (Exodus 24:5–8)

The blood of young bulls was sprinkled on the people to confirm the Sinai Covenant between God and Israel. Unfortunately, the Israelites failed to keep it. However, God knew from the very beginning that mankind would not be able to live a righteous life in which they would not fall from their perfect state, just like Adam and Eve did. So from the very beginning, as is made clear in Genesis 3, God promised that He would send a perfect Lamb to pay this price, restoring the covenant of righteousness (i.e., the Sinai Covenant) back to mankind.

But this restored righteousness was not going to be gained through the works or deeds of people, but rather by the works of the Son of God, Yeshua. As you have already discerned, we will refer to this covenant — which only Yeshua was able to qualify for — as the Sinai Covenant, which is called the Old Covenant in the New Testament.

Yeshua's life, death, and resurrection prove this very point. Yeshua did not gain His righteousness via faith; He gained it by living a perfect life. Remember, He was part God and part man, which made Him an inheritor of the sinful nature. But he did not succumb to temptation like the rest of us.

> When He said, "A new *covenant*," He has made the first obsolete. But whatever is becoming obsolete and growing old is ready to disappear. (Hebrews 8:13)

> But to the one who does not work, but believes in Him who justifies the ungodly, his faith is credited as righteousness . . . (Romans 4:5)

This New Covenant of righteousness is the second way that people may be saved, or made righteous, or put back in good standing with God. As we have learned, this New Covenant comes through faith, not through works or deeds. This is the primary difference between the two covenants above. Now, instead of working our way to righteousness we have a New Covenant that allows us to enter into this covenant of righteousness through faith. The following verses all support the above, but are usually misunderstood.

> And in the same way *He took* the cup after they had eaten, saying, "This cup which is poured out for you is the new covenant in My blood. (Luke 22:20)

The Sinai Covenant was confirmed by sprinkling the blood of young bulls on the people of Israel. The New Covenant is made by the shed blood of our Lord, and we confirm it by drinking wine or grape juice, Yeshua's shed blood's representation, at our Passover Seders. The Christians know this as communion.

> "THIS IS MY COVENANT WITH THEM,
> WHEN I TAKE AWAY THEIR SINS." (Romans 11:27)

The New Covenant takes away sin, which involves violation of the Laws of God. It does not take away the Laws of God, just the penalty for violating those Laws.

> Who also made us adequate *as* servants of a new covenant, not of the letter but of the Spirit; for the letter kills, but the Spirit gives life. (2 Corinthians 3:6)

The letter (Law) kills us but the Spirit gives life. The consequence of violating the Sinai Covenant was death, for mankind cannot keep from sinning. But the New Covenant now can restore righteousness through faith.

> But their minds were hardened; for until this very day at the reading of the old covenant the same veil remains unlifted, because it is removed in Christ. (2 Corinthians 3:14)

The Sinai Covenant is removed, not the Law. Just the consequence of failing under the old covenant — death — is removed.

> So much the more also Jesus has become the guarantee of a better covenant. (Hebrews 7:22)

The New Covenant is better because we can qualify under the new one.

> For if that first *covenant* had been faultless, there would have been no occasion sought for a second. (Hebrews 8:7)

The Sinai Covenant is "faulty" because we can't qualify and adhere to it. The text is not saying that the Law is not holy or faulty, only that the portion of the covenant that required us to obey the Law was faulty. In fact, maybe it's not even that the covenant itself was faulty, but the ones who made it with God were faulty.

As we said above with respect to Hebrew 8:13, the covenant that required us to obey the Law is obsolete, not the Law itself.

> Now the God of peace, who brought up from the dead the great Shepherd of the sheep through the blood of the eternal covenant, *even* Jesus our Lord, 21equip you in every good thing to do His will, working in us that which is pleasing in His sight, through Jesus Christ, to whom *be* the glory forever and ever. Amen. (Hebrews 13:20–21)

Praise God, the New Covenant is eternal. It cannot be destroyed by our sin.

> You foolish Galatians, who has bewitched you, before whose eyes Jesus Christ was publicly portrayed *as* crucified? 2 This is the only thing I want to find out from you: did you receive the Spirit by the works of the Law, or by hearing with faith? 3 Are you so foolish? Having begun by the Spirit, are you now being perfected by the flesh? 4 Did you suffer so many things in vain — if indeed it was in vain? 5 So then, does He who provides you with the Spirit and works miracles among you, do it by the works of the Law, or by hearing with faith?

> 6 Even so Abraham BELIEVED GOD, AND IT WAS RECKONED TO HIM AS RIGHTEOUSNESS. 7 Therefore, be sure that it is those who are of faith who are sons of Abraham. 8 The Scripture, foreseeing that God would justify the Gentiles by faith, preached the gospel beforehand to Abraham, *saying*, "ALL THE NATIONS WILL BE BLESSED IN YOU." 9 So then those who are of faith are blessed with Abraham, the believer.

> 10 For as many as are of the works of the Law are under a curse; for it is written, "CURSED IS EVERYONE WHO DOES NOT ABIDE BY ALL THINGS WRITTEN IN THE BOOK OF

THE LAW, TO PERFORM THEM." [11] Now that no one is justified by the Law before God is evident; for, "THE RIGHTEOUS MAN SHALL LIVE BY FAITH." [12] However, the Law is not of faith; on the contrary, "HE WHO PRACTICES THEM SHALL LIVE BY THEM." [13] Christ redeemed us from the curse of the Law, having become a curse for us — for it is written, "CURSED IS EVERYONE WHO HANGS ON A TREE" — [14] in order that in Christ Jesus the blessing of Abraham might come to the Gentiles, so that we would receive the promise of the Spirit through faith.

[15] Brethren, I speak in terms of human relations: even though it is *only* a man's covenant, yet when it has been ratified, no one sets it aside or adds conditions to it. [16] Now the promises were spoken to Abraham and to his seed. He does not say, "And to seeds," as *referring* to many, but *rather* to one, "And to your seed," that is, Christ. [17] What I am saying is this: the Law, which came four hundred and thirty years later, does not invalidate a covenant previously ratified by God, so as to nullify the promise. [18] For if the inheritance is based on law, it is no longer based on a promise; but God has granted it to Abraham by means of a promise.

[19] Why the Law then? It was added because of transgressions, having been ordained through angels by the agency of a mediator, until the seed would come to whom the promise had been made. [20] Now a mediator is not for one *party only*; whereas God is *only* one. [21] Is the Law then contrary to the promises of God? May it never be! For if a law had been given which was able to impart life, then righteousness would indeed have been based on law. [22] But the Scripture has shut up everyone under sin, so that the promise by faith in Jesus Christ might be given to those who believe.

[23] But before faith came, we were kept in custody under the law, being shut up to the faith which was later to be

revealed. [24] Therefore the Law has become our tutor *to lead us* to Christ, so that we may be justified by faith. (Galatians 3:1–24)

In this chapter the word interpreted as *justified* means *righteous*. Paul explains our position perfectly here. In the New Covenant, righteousness is procured by faith, not by works of the Law as in the Sinai Covenant. By the Sinai Covenant we are cursed, and no one is made righteous by that covenant except our Messiah.

Three Primary Covenants

In the Bible, there are three fundamental covenants that God made with mankind. We are not talking about the covenants that we have explained in our other writings, which include servanthood, friendship, inheritance, and the bridal covenant. Here we are referring to the Sinai Covenant, made around 1400 B.C., and the New Covenant, made when Yeshua died on the cross and rose from the dead, and paid the price for our sin around 2,000 years ago.

But the third covenant, which was actually the first covenant made, precedes both of the other two, occurring somewhere around 2100 B.C. We will call it the *Abrahamic Covenant*. It is described more fully in Genesis 15, where God shed blood by splitting some animals in half and making a promise to Abraham that his descendants would be as many as the stars in the heavens, and that he would inherit the Promised Land, as well as inherit righteousness through faith.

All three of these covenants are represented and confirmed by the shedding of blood. They all build on one another.

- In the first, God promises to Abraham that He will be the father of many nations, but also that he would inherit righteousness through faith.

- In the second, God offers the same gift — righteousness — but this time by following the Law.

- In the third, because God knew from the foundations of the Earth that mankind could not follow the terms of the second covenant, He sent His Son to live a perfect live per the Sinai Covenant, thus shedding His blood as payment for our failures.

This is all prophesied within the Abrahamic Covenant. The Abrahamic Covenant promises that a seed shall come that will restore righteousness to mankind. The fact that Abraham will have an offspring verified the fact that this seed that Paul refers to as the Messiah, Yeshua, in Galatians, will guarantee that Abraham and his descendants shall be inheritors of the family of God. God shall become One with mankind through inserting Himself into the family of Abraham and his descendants. This is the reason why the New Testament refers to salvation as being born again. We are born into this new family when we trust and rely and have faith in the promise of the Abrahamic Covenant.

God wanted us to inherit His promise that He gave to Abraham, so this promise becomes the promise of the inheritance of the first born and is represented as the promise of salvation in the New Covenant. The Law was added because of our sin until the promised One would come.

In verse 21 it says that the Law is not contrary to the promises of God. The Law did not bring righteousness, only faith in Yeshua. The Law acted as a tutor that would lead us to God. Because God is righteous and holy, these instructions lead us into holiness when we follow the Laws of God and behave like our King. Thus, when He came, we could easily identify Him.

These passages are used to promote the idea that the Sinai Covenant, understood by some as "the Law," has been abolished and replaced by a new and better covenant. However, the better understanding is that these verses bring us a better covenant because we are unable to qualify for righteousness under the Sinai Covenant. And only under the New Covenant are we able to become righteous by faith. The Law has not been abolished; only the Sinai Covenant that promised to make us righteous by obeying the Law was abolished.

However, *in actuality I'm not so sure that anything has been abolished, because covenants can't be abolished*. What may actually be occurring in regard to these covenants is that, because of Yeshua's death on the cross as payment for our sins and our violations of the covenant, we now become white as snow. We become holy, not by our own works but by faith in the works of Yeshua. Thus, God sees our sins no more. They are separated as far as the east is from the west.

Qualifying Under the Sinai Covenant

So, what are we saying? There are two ways to inherit the promise of eternal life via righteousness. One comes by being totally obedient to the requirements of the Sinai Covenant by living a life in total accord with the Laws of God. The second way to inherit this same promise of righteousness and eternal life is by faith in the "Good News," the gospel of Yeshua.

The New Covenant was created from the very beginning because God knew that mankind would not be able to live a perfect life, as His Son did. So He made the New Covenant with mankind that allowed righteousness to come through faith. But this very New Covenant was prophesied in the first covenant, the Abrahamic Covenant, when God referred to the Seed that would come.

Now let's get to our last point. In the following verse it says that an angel appeared who had the eternal gospel:

> And I saw another angel flying in midheaven, having an eternal gospel to preach to those who live on the

earth, and to every nation and tribe and tongue and people. (Revelation 14:6)

The word for eternal here means "without beginning or end — it has always been and shall always be." The word "gospel" in our passage means "glad tidings and good news." In the Old and New Testaments this word describes the promise that the kingdom of God will be set up and that salvation and righteousness come through faith in Yeshua.

But you may be asking yourself, "Where has the Gospel been preached other than in the New Testament? Isn't the idea of the good news a New Testament concept only?" Here are two verses from the Old Testament:

Sing to the Lord, bless His name, proclaim good tidings of His salvation from day to day. (Psalm 96:2)

How lovely on the mountains are the feet of him who brings good news, Who announces peace and brings good news of happiness, Who announces salvation and says to Zion, Your God Reigns. (Isaiah 52:7)

These passages, along with many more, refer to good news and good tidings of this same promise of salvation. The same Hebrew word, *basar*, underlines both the New Testament and Old Testament passages concerning this good news. It is just that in the Old Testament this word gets translated as *good news or tidings*, while the English word *Gospel* is chosen in the New Testament.

As we can see, the good news was proposed right from the very beginning, in Genesis 3. The power of God shone through, building onto this Good News, via the Abrahamic Covenant that was revealed in Genesis 15.

In the passage below Paul confirms this everlasting Gospel when he says that God even preached the Gospel to Abraham.

> Even so Abraham BELIEVED GOD, AND IT WAS RECKONED TO HIM AS RIGHTEOUSNESS. 7 Therefore, be sure that it is those who are of faith who are sons of Abraham. 8 The Scripture, foreseeing that God would justify the Gentiles by faith, preached the gospel beforehand to Abraham, *saying*, "ALL THE NATIONS WILL BE BLESSED IN YOU." 9 So then those who are of faith are blessed with Abraham, the believer. (Galatians 3:6–9)

The reference to God's "preaching" clearly is referring to Genesis 15 in the context of the Abrahamic Covenant. The Bible comes to a conclusion with the completion of the promises, and the means to achieve the promises of the Abrahamic Covenant.

Thus the Bible is one complete panoramic view of the plan of God. This plan has as its focus the means for the restoration of mankind back to his original righteous state in the family of God. And in order for us to look like we're in the family of God, God means for us to be holy, because He is holy and He wants us so very much to be in His family . . . and to look like we truly belong there.

Footnotes

1 http://en.wikipedia.org/wiki/Tora! Tora! Tora!

2 David Biven and Roy Blizzard, Jr., *Understanding the Difficult Words of Jesus*, Revised Edition (Destiny Image Publishers, Inc., 2001)

Other Books at Lostintranslation.org

Lost in Translation: Rediscovering the Hebrew Roots of our Faith *(Volume 1)*

John Klein and Adam Spears

Despite the sensational nature of its subject, *Lost in Translation: Rediscovering the Hebrew Roots of our Faith* is written in simple, clear, rational language that relies 100 percent on the Bible as the ultimate authority.

The authors shed light on centuries of confusion surrounding subjects that are seldom addressed in modern sermons and Bible studies. Using ancient Hebrew language and culture, they clarify many of the Bible's so-called "mysteries" and help the reader uncover the treasure of foundational truths that have been "lost in translation." Topics include:

- Who is the Bride of Messiah?

- Is there a difference between covenant and testament?

- How does the rainbow reflect God's plan for mankind?

- What is the difference between devils, demons, and nephilim?

Join us on an exciting adventure to rediscover the treasures still buried within the pages of The Book that reveal the pathway to the heart of God.

Lost in Translation: The Book of Revelation Through Hebrew Eyes
(Volume 2)

John Klein and Adam Spears

The Book of Revelation through Hebrew Eyes is the second in the Lost in Translation three-volume series.

The title says it all! This book takes a look at the first half of the book of Revelation from its Hebraic cultural and linguistic perspective. The truth of many misunderstood verses will be revealed when the light of ancient Hebrew interpretation is shone on the Bible's premiere book of end-times prophecy. Many intriguing questions will be answered, such as:

- Who are the 144,000?

- Are all believers the Bride of Messiah?

- What are the locusts that come from the abyss?

If you're interested in this volume, we highly recommend reading the first volume, because it lays the foundation for understanding the book of Revelation.

Lost in Translation: The Book of Revelation: Two Brides — Two Destinies *(Volume 3)*

John Klein and Adam Spears

In the final volume of this series the authors explore the second half of Revelation from the perspective of a Hebrew God speaking through a Hebrew believer to an audience that was intimately familiar with the Hebrew language, culture, customs, and concepts that form both the literal and metaphorical foundation for vast portions of Revelation. In the process they answer a multitude of important questions, including:

- Whose bride are you? Can you change sides or are you stuck forever in a relationship you really don't want?

- Who or what is the False Messiah? The False Prophet?

- What is the Second Death?

- Could these catastrophes happen in my lifetime?

It is especially important for the current generation to understand the Bible's premiere book on end-times prophecy because deception will be rampant.

Anatomy of the Heavens, God's Message in the Stars

John Klein

The constellations in our night sky have captivated almost everyone throughout history and have a remarkable story to tell. It's God's most dramatic message, and it's literally written in the stars. Each of the 12 constellations plays its part in telling the overarching plan God has had since the beginning of creation.

Although Satan has used astrology to pervert God's purpose for the stars, God has provided the starry hosts to fulfill the reason for their creation. The stars were originally created for signs (Genesis 1:14) — signs that link to biblical prophecy.

Each of the 12 tribes is represented and embellished by one of the constellations. Amazingly, the position of the stars during the biblical festivals also gives insight into God's grand plan.

Daniel Roars Today — End Times Prophecies Affecting You

John Klein

Daniel Roars because it's a message that must be heard today. It's a message received 2,600 years ago, but it was meant for our time, especially as the end of the ages draws near.

Daniel is one of the rare biblical individuals about whom God has nothing but good things to say. That may be why Daniel was chosen to convey the largest apocalyptic section of Scripture in the Old Testament. The book of Revelation cannot be understood properly without the foundation Daniel provides.

As Daniel's prophesies roar in our ears they create a longing in our hearts, for the arrival of the groom. Deciphering Daniel helps prepare us for the most important even in history.

Biblical Nuggets

John Klein

Get rich in the only way that really matters. Looking at the Scriptures from an Hebraic perspective turns up real treasures of the best kind — nuggets that are golden because of how they affect your life and your understanding of God's word. In this book they fall into seven categories:

- Personal Relationships with God
- Science and the Bible
- Biblical History
- Biblical Feasts
- From an Hebraic Perspective
- Hebrew Language and Pictographs
- End Times

Flip to your favorite areas of interest and start mining. We promise . . . you'll strike Gold.

Family Sabbath Seder

Jodi Klein

The Family Sabbath Seder makes it easy for you and your family to join together in marking the beginning and closing of Sabbath, setting it off as the best day of the week. The Seder contains well-thought-out gems that have been developed by people over the centuries to aid in keeping the fourth commandment. Candle lighting, wine, bread, and havdalah blessings are in easy-to-read Hebrew transliterations so your family can correctly pronounce the Hebrew if you decide to use the Hebrew blessings.

Our tried-and-true favorite hallah bread recipes are included (with one for bread machines!), along with a question-and-answer page geared to pointing out that everything you do in welcoming the Sabbath is imbued with meaning.

The Family Sabbath Seder makes it easy to establish rich traditions that will continue for generations.

Couple's Sabbath Seder

Jodi Klein

This Seder is a tool for couples to use in welcoming the Sabbath. Included are candle lighting, wine, bread, and havdalah blessings in easy-to-read Hebrew transliterations and our favorite hallah bread recipes.

The Seder will fulfill any couple's desire to please God by marking the opening and closing of the Sabbath in this special way.

Single's Sabbath Seder

Jodi Klein

Begin your Sabbath by reflecting on God with these time-honored traditions adapted specifically for the single person. You're invited to meet with Him as His special day arrives, and a tradition of using the Sabbath Seder can enrich that intimate weekly appointment.

Hanukkah Covenant Seder

Jodi Klein

This family-friendly Seder takes you through the eight nights of Hanukkah by beginning with a Hebrew blessing centering on Yeshua and transliterated phonetically so that even those unfamiliar with Hebrew can read it accurately.

This Seder is unique in that it uses color to teach about covenant and to answer the question, "How do I draw near to God?" Each night includes sections on covenant, relevant scriptures, enrichment, and the history of Hanukkah, enabling kids and adults to understand covenant and what it means to have a relationship with the Light of the

World. This 60-page booklet is chock full of suggestions to make your Hanukkah more meaningful than ever.

S'firat HaOmer: Counting the Omer

Jodi Klein

Leviticus 23:15, 16 instructs us to count the omer. How do we do that? This book makes it simple, with one page for each day of the count. The short blessing and the count are in Hebrew and English, with easy-to-pronounce phonetic Hebrew. Counting the Omer is 100% user-friendly - if you can read English, you can correctly pronounce the Hebrew transliteration!

We have not seen another book that makes it so easy for you to fulfill the Leviticus 23: 15, 16 command, and you'll end up learning some Hebrew while you're at it.

Why did God instruct us to count up seven weeks to Shavuot beginning on the festival of Firstfruits? Because the wheat harvest, Shavuot, is the best harvest and represents the Groom's harvest of the Bride. There's going to be a wedding! Shavuot (Pentecost in Greek) represents the Hebrew custom of the snatching of the Bride prior to the wedding.

Counting the Omer is the intense anticipation God built into this particular holiday by requiring us to count the days leading up to it.

The Key to Your Weather Forecast

John Klein

Today, talk of the current weather forecast is one of the most common but least understood topics. This book will cut through all the confusion and allow anyone to make an accurate weather forecast. Used in a remote outdoor location or just around town, this field guide will enable you to quickly acquire an understanding of what causes the dramatic weather changes, which we all talk about, and make your own exciting predictions.

This key has been designed to make weather forecasting fun and easy and distinguishes this book from every other on the subject. Without the need for prior instruction or aid, you can determine the weather by answering the simple questions in the key.

The promise: this book will enable you to accurately forecast the weather for the next few days in about 5 minutes.

30754974R00068